GUIDANCE MONOGRAPH SERIES

SHELLEY C. STONE

BRUCE SHERTZER

Editors

GUIDANCE MONOGRAPH SERIES

The general purpose of Houghton Mifflin's Guidance Monograph Series is to provide high quality coverage of topics which are of abiding importance in contemporary counseling and guidance practice. In a rapidly expanding field of endeavor, change and innovation are inevitably present. A trend accompanying such growth is greater and greater specialization. Specialization results in an increased demand for materials which reflect current modifications in guidance practice while simultaneously treating the field in greater depth and detail than commonly found in textbooks and brief journal articles.

The list of eminent contributors to this series assures the reader expert treatment of the areas covered. The monographs are designed for consumers with varying familiarity to the counseling and guidance field. The editors believe that the series will be useful to experienced practitioners as well as beginning students. While these groups may use the monographs with somewhat different goals in mind, both will benefit from the treatment given to content areas.

The content areas treated have been selected because of specific criteria. Among them are timeliness, practicality, and persistency of the issues involved. Above all, the editors have attempted to select topics which are of major substantive concern to counseling and guidance personnel.

Shelley C. Stone

Bruce Shertzer

THEORIES OF OCCUPATIONAL CHOICE AND VOCATIONAL DEVELOPMENT

JOSEPH S. ZACCARIA
UNIVERSITY OF ILLINOIS

HOUGHTON MIFFLIN COMPANY · BOSTON
NEW YORK · ATLANTA · GENEVA, ILL. · DALLAS · PALO ALTO

CONTENTS

EDITORS' INTRODUCTION

Most American youth engage in three fundamental processes that produce immediate and residual impact upon their lives. These include 1) the development and/or refinement of a set of values (philosophy of life) that will be used to resolve many decisions and issues still before them, 2) a career choice and 3) the choice of a marriage partner. Reflection upon these processes leads to the notion that the three are concerned with the why of life, how life will be used and with whom life is to be spent. Further, each process interacts and influences others.

This monograph presents an overview of the major theories of vocational choice and development. The vocational development of students has long been and still remains a major undertaking of school counselors. And rightly so. The counselor who would help students in vocational development must possess some understanding of the factors which bear upon them as they move toward choice.

The past few years have yielded several theories or approaches which seek to explain vocational choice and development. Some of these approaches have gained prominence and won general acceptance by counseling practitioners because they serve as a framework against which they can base their conceptions, clarify their thoughts and actions, and deepen their understanding of the processes and procedures. But above all, theories are useful to the counselor who seeks to be helpful to an individual engaged in clarifying his view of himself and his decision-making processes.

In this monograph, Professor Zaccaria presents some formulations of work and its influence upon individuals. He outlines the contributions and speculations of various disciplines toward work. Further, Zaccaria ably describes the function of theory to the practitioner and maps out the work of contemporary vocational development theorists. Finally, the author has sought to explain the meaning of theory building to the practitioner and has provided examples of practical applications of theories at different school levels. For these reasons we believe this monograph will be useful to guidance personnel.

Shelley C. Stone
Bruce E. Shertzer

AUTHOR'S INTRODUCTION

As the field of counseling and guidance has moved into a period of its development roughly analogous to that of adolescence, its search for an identity has been accompanied by a surge in the area of theory building. Paradigms, formulations, approaches, models, stances, theoretical orientations, and the like have come to occupy an increasingly more central role in the functioning of both theoreticians and practitioners. The emergence of more sophisticated approaches to guidance is clearly evident in the implementation of guidance services, pupil personnel services, and the various developmental strategies. The recent refinement and extension of counseling theory and techniques, coupled with advances in vocational development theories and the practices of vocational guidance constitute dual thrusts for operationalizing more effective guidance programs. Traditional oversimplifications, such as the familiar educational/vocational/personal-social trichotomy, and the presentation of issues in terms of simplified either/or positions have given way to more enlightened perspectives regarding the nature of the individual and the most effective procedures for providing him with preventive and remedial assistance.

Providing help in making more adequate decisions relating to the world of work has been a continuing theme of the counseling and guidance movement since its inception. Indeed, it was largely because of the increased complexity of the occupational structure and the resultant difficulties of occupational choice, problems of vocational adjustment, loss of talent, etc., that the counseling and guidance movement came into being. During its history, counseling and guidance has grown from a largely informal effort to a young profession attempting to provide youth and adults with highly sophisticated forms of assistance. During the intervening period of time, the structure of the world of work and the very meaning of work have undergone significant evolution and revolution. Also, since the birth of the counseling and guidance movement shortly after the turn of the century, the role and function of the practitioner have undergone vast changes.

The bases for the work of the practitioners have had to be altered in light of new advances in theory building and the systematic derivation of practice from a well-articulated professional stance. Thus, practices stemming from bases such as tradition, authority, whim, trial and error, intuition, etc., have been replaced increasingly by practices built upon a knowledgeable and sensitive understanding derived from systematic inquiry. At the heart of this systematic inquiry are theory and research. A number of philosophical and operational positions have been proposed whereby various stances and general strategies can be implemented in the work of the practitioner.

Work can be a significant facet of life. Certainly it defines our existence as no other activity can. It can be a source for success, satisfaction, and pride. It can be a source of worry, concern, and general maladjustment. It is the purpose of this monograph to survey the field of occupational choice and vocational development theory and to appraise the usefulness of this theory as an aid to work of the practitioner. Vocational development and vocational development theory, however, are relevant not only to the professional counselor but also to teachers, clergy, school administrators, and parents. Whether an individual views work as a way of life, an implementation of the self-concept, a curse, a duty, an expression of love, or a means for individual, family, or national survival, the centrality of work and the importance of adequate vocational development demands that all who provide helping relationships be sensitive to the importance of work in our lives. This book is dedicated to those who have labored at vocational theory building and is intended for those who help others in their vocational development.

JOSEPH SALVATORE ZACCARIA

1

Occupational Choice and Vocational Development

One of the major dilemmas of the practitioner is that of knowing what is the best procedure for helping an individual. An adequately prepared guidance worker certainly has a wide range of available techniques available to him for achieving his goals. Counseling, testing, case study, group guidance, consultation, sociometry, referral, occupational information, bibliotherapy, and the case conference represent a few of the many procedures at the disposal of the practitioner. The problem of what constitutes the best strategy for helping any given person, however, is further complicated by mediating factors such as the practitioner's frame of reference, the setting in which the help is provided, the needs of the client, the organizational structure and policies of the institution, and the inherent financial and physical limitations of the context in which the practitioner works. The goals of guidance have continued to be broad, lofty, and noble. While further refinement of guidance techniques and helping relationships in general is desirable, present approaches are sufficiently useful for helping the troubled person to provide an effective base for the work of the practitioner. Each of the procedures listed above constitutes a potential vehicle for achieving the goals of the guidance worker.

The basic dimensions of the practitioner's "problem of knowing" include (a) knowing himself, (b) knowing the nature of the client, (c) knowing the range of potential goals for the process of guidance, and (d) knowing the available techniques for achieving any given goal. Four ways of knowing have been identified (Ianni, 1967). The first way of knowing is the method of tenacity. This has been called the "We hold these truths to be self-evident" or "In our hearts we know we are right" approach. The second method of knowing is the method of authority, the "Forty million Frenchmen can't be wrong" or the "You can be sure if it's Westinghouse" approach. A third method of knowing is the *a priori* or intuitive method. "It stands to reason" or "Let's sit down and reason together" typify this method of knowing. Lastly, there is the method of science. Whereas other approaches for knowing are based upon tradition, whim, trial and error, authority, intuition, or speculation, the method of science is based upon external permanency. Each of the above methods has been used by guidance practitioners to deal with their problem of knowing. Implicitly or explicitly every practitioner has used one of the above approaches for knowing. Both the goals and the available techniques are too numerous for a practitioner to glibly state that he will seek to implement all of the goals of guidance through the use of all available procedures. Too many goals have been stated. Too many techniques have been offered. The practitioner must choose. He should have an adequate way of choosing. He should have an adequate way of "knowing" before he chooses. The theme of this monograph is as follows: to as great an extent as possible, the practice of counseling and guidance should be derived from (a) an understanding of the practitioner's own personality and professional goals (tempered by pragmatic factors in the work setting) and (b) an understanding of the relevant theory and research. The method of science, i.e., scientific inquiry, thus constitutes a vehicle for knowing. Theories of occupational choice and vocational development represent the results of attempts to know how people choose jobs and function within the world of work. These theories offer a perspective for knowing how to help clients with vocational problems. Thus, theory represents a possible basis for the work of the guidance practitioner. If this position is taken, then the old myth concerning the irrelevancy and impracticability of theory becomes a belief in the statement that nothing is as useful as a good theory.

The Nature and Place of Theory in Guidance

The nature of theory has long been of interest to philosophers, scientists, and academicians. A major shortcoming in the education of most guidance practitioners is that theories in general have been studied apart from their implications and applications in work settings. Listed below are some definitions of the term theory:

> A general principle, supported by considerable data, proposed as an explanation of a group of phenomena; a statement of the relations believed to prevail in a comprehensive body of facts. A theory is more solidly supported by evidence than a hypothesis. It is less firmly established than a law, which is usually limited to a single kind of relationship (English and English, 1958, p. 197).
>
> . . . a set of ideas so related to each other that they account for or explain a set of facts (Broudy, 1961, pp. 16–17).
>
> . . . an unsubstantiated hypothesis or speculation concerning reality which is not yet definitely known to be so (Hall and Lindzey, 1957, p. 10).
>
> . . . a human convention for keeping data in order . . . a provisional systemization of events (Stefflre, 1965, pp. 1–2).
>
> . . . a conceptual model to explain a process inferred from observed behavior (McCabe, 1958, p. 49).
>
> . . . a possible world which can be checked against the real world (Pepinsky and Pepinsky, 1954, p. 18).

The functions of theory include the following:

1. Keeps data in order.
2. Reduces complexities to manageable proportions.
3. Tells the practitioner what to look for, what to expect, and where to go.
4. Leads to the observation of relationships which might have been previously overlooked.
5. Defines operational truths.
6. Focuses attention on relevant data by telling what to look for.
7. Leads to the use of consistent terminology.
8. Helps to construct new methods of behaving.
9. Leads to useful generalizations.
10. Aids in seeing sense and meaning in other people's behavior.

An Anthropological Perspective on Work

Anthropology has traditionally been defined as the science of man. This discipline, the most comprehensive of the behavioral sciences, studies all men, in all places, during all periods of man's biological, psychological, and sociocultural development. The two sub-fields of anthropology which are most relevant to occupational choice and vocational development are cultural anthropology and economic anthropology. Cultural anthropology deals with the patterning of human behavior resulting from the culture in which man develops. The field of economic anthropology studies the tools and techniques of production, designates the means and level of subsistence within cultures, and analyzes social relationships which involve the amount and distribution of goods and services in a culture. The central concept in the field of anthropology is culture. In their classical study Kroeber and Kluckholm (1952) found 257 definitions of the term culture and arranged them into a taxonomy of seven groups each of which views culture somewhat differently. Titiev (1963) identifies the following three axioms in the field of cultural anthropology: (a) a total society has a distinct existence, quite apart from that of any of the individuals of whom it is composed, (b) every society seeks to perpetuate itself biologically through the birth of offspring to its members, and (c) every society strives to continue its patterns of culture indefinitely through teaching infants to know and accept its ways of life. The school with its curriculum (including counseling and guidance) represents our culture's major institution for transmitting our culture to youth. Through patterning (socialization), the behavior of the individual is made more orderly and predictable and what results is a generalized type of behavior known as modal personality, configurational personality, basic personality, or national character. In the broadest sense of the term, culture is not behavior per se, but rather an abstraction of the collective behavior of a group of people sharing certain commonalities. Similarly, the concepts of basic personality, modal personality, etc. are abstractions of behavioral propensities evident among members of a given culture. The writer has summarized the implications of culture and of culture and personality theory as it relates to the general work of the practitioner, noting that these concepts, like many of those in other behavioral sciences, provide a global perspective and a backdrop for the goals and the role and function of the practitioner (Zaccaria, 1967). The components of culture or the cultural scheme include the following: (a) speech, (b) art, (c) mythology and religion, (d) religious practices, (e) family and social systems, (f) property, (g) government, (h) war, and (i) material traits. Work is part of the cultural scheme because occupations and industries are a portion of the material traits aspect of culture. Thus, the preparation for an occupation, the process of entering an occupation, the patterns of work and the products or services of work constitute a part of the total matrix of our American culture.

Changes in the world of work such as changes in the occupational structure, technological innovations, work patterns, work values, and the inherent meaning of work represent a part of the more pervasive process of cultural change in twentieth century America. For example, the recent changes and proposed changes in regard to the role and function of women in the world of work reflect the more general cultural change with respect to the proper place of women in our culture. Many aspects of work and work related activities, while typical of our culture, vary greatly when viewed against the panorama of all of the world cultures. Anthropology describes the various types of community structures, family patterns, and economic systems which greatly influence occupational choice and work. Viewed within an anthropological perspective, work may be viewed as part of the larger process of enculturation. Enculturation is the process of adjusting an individual's responses increasingly to a society's patterns of culture . . . [it] "may be regarded as the manner in which each society molds the genetically controlled organization of its neonates to a set of pre-existing cultural norms." (Titiev, 1963, p. 484) Hopefully, individuals will interiorize (introject) the cultural values of the society and in so doing become well-adjusted.

A Sociological Perspective on Work

The field of sociology focuses upon man's group life and the products of his group living. Within the broad field of sociology there are two sub-fields which are particularly relevant to vocational development theory — industrial sociology and occupational sociology. In general, a sociological view of work emphasizes the structure and dynamics of the various types of social organizations within which work occurs. Both the organizations and the lives of workers within these organizations provide the subject matter of industrial sociology. Specifically, industrial sociology deals with the following:

1. Work groups and work relations.
2. The role the worker plays in work groups.
3. The structure and dynamics of complex organizations.
4. The relation of industry to the local community.
5. The patterns and values of an industrial society. (Miller, 1964)

Occupational sociology deals with the following areas:

1. The social nature of work and related phenomena such as leisure, play, recreation, retirement, unemployment, etc.
2. The analysis of the occupational structure.

3. The study of individual occupations.
4. The articulation of the occupational structure with other segments of society.
5. The study of a particular occupation to highlight an important problem in the broader society. (Nosow and Form, 1962)

In general, sociology has provided counseling and guidance with a rich background of data, demographic studies, descriptive studies of various occupations, together with a global orientation to the place of the worker in the social organization of the work setting and an understanding of the general place of work in our society. While there are two theories of occupational choice which have evolved from the field of sociology, neither of these theories has been widely accepted or influential upon the field of counseling and guidance. Thus, the contributions of sociology have continued to be those of providing an understanding of the parameters of the meaning of work in our society and offering a general backdrop against which the insights of other disciplines could be highlighted. In light of the general forces which generate sociocultural phenomena, Borow (1966) has identified a number of general areas of study which are closely related to the process of occupational choice. These areas include socioeconomic status, occupational prestige, level or aspiration, level of occupational choice, differences among rural-urban groups, institutional pressures, the influence of parents and other significant persons, cultural deprivation, and various social precipitants of occupational choice, e.g., outside work experience, school studies, societal trends, etc.

One of the theories of occupational choice to come from the field of sociology is the theory of occupational inheritance. In some instances family pressures and social influences act upon the individual in such a way that the individual is coerced into following the occupation of the father. Ironically, this theory of occupational choice involves no choice or at best, choice by default.

Two basically different patterns of occupational inheritance have been described (Caplow, 1954; Gross, 1958, 1964). In the phenomenon of occupational transmission, the father transmits the occupation of the individual largely through deliberate indoctrination. The instruction occurs in such areas as beliefs, customs, required skills, etc. of that occupation. Thus, for example, a father who owns a business may inculcate values and through family pressure attempt to insure the transmission of the business to the son by influencing the son's occupational choice. The pattern of occupational transmission or occupational succession occurs largely in such job fields as farming, mining, business proprietorship, and in some professions. The second type of occupational inheritance is known as forced inheritance and is prevalent among the disadvantaged where the son may actually be restricted in his occupational choice by virtue of social and/or economic factors related to membership in the lower socioeconomic strata of society. In general, the amount of occupational inheritance appears to have diminished largely because of greater educational opportunity and increased geographical and social mobility.

Miller and Form (1949) have contributed both a theory of occupational choice and some concepts which have become vital components of other theorists' formulations. Their theory of occupational choice stresses the importance of accident. Such factors as time of birth, place of birth, race, nationality, social class, place of residence, parental expectations, influence of relatives, and peer influences are all accidental and greatly influence the nature of the occupation which the individual selects. Many of the above factors also greatly influence the individual's educational and cultural opportunities. While most theorists would accept the notion that there are many chance or accidental factors which have a bearing on occupational choice and the course of career development, Miller and Form have perhaps overestimated the helplessness of the individual and have tended to overlook the fact that for counselors, a focus on the individual is more desirable than the determination of typical or modal behavior followed by gross generalizations about groups of people. Miller and Form have contributed two important concepts for other theory builders — work stages and career patterns. They identify three major work periods in the lives of individuals. First there is an initial work period which includes all of the part-time and full-time jobs held by individuals up to the time they complete their formal education. The trial work period typically follows the initial work period. What occurs at this stage is "shopping around," training jobs, or the general exploration of several jobs, each of which is held only for a short period of time (three years or less). Finally, there can be a stable work period in which the individual appears to have settled down and stabilizes in a job for three years or more. Two other work stages include the preparatory stage (childhood) and the retirement stage (late adulthood). In their analysis of case histories of 276 individuals, Miller and Form identified fourteen basic patterns of work periods in which there were seven secure career patterns and seven insecure career patterns.

A Philosophical Perspective on Work

Philosophy literally means the love of wisdom. Aristotle's famous statement, "All men by nature desire to know," symbolizes the traditional thinking of Western civilization in regard to our continuing search for knowledge, understanding and wisdom. The sub-areas within philosophy which are most relevant for counseling and guidance are cosmology (the study of man in the universe), epistemology (the study of the nature of truth), and axiology (the study of value and of what in man is worthwhile). Each of these sub-fields seeks to add a different dimension to man's search for wisdom. Although the nature of wisdom varies from culture to culture and varies perhaps even within a given culture from one historical period to another, philosophy in Western civilization has typically dealt with certain fundamental questions. The significance of these questions and the alternative answers to the questions are immediately apparent in terms of the process of counseling and guidance.

1. The meaning of human existence.
2. The significance of the world in which man finds himself.
3. The general nature of the universe in which human life has its setting.
4. The nature of man's destiny in the universe.
5. The extent to which man can affect the universe by his actions.
6. The nature of man.
7. The behaviors man should choose.
8. The type of individual and collective life that is most worthwhile learning and living. (Beck, 1963)

Specifically, the formal philosophical systems can make an indirect contribution to a more adequate understanding of occupational choice, career development, work, etc. by illuminating the most basic questions of what is the nature of the universe, the nature of man, and the fundamental relationship between man and the broad universe. The nature of worthwhile work, the relationship of work to leisure, the meaning of work, the place of work in the total spectrum of man's life, etc. constitute some of the relevant issues which can be answered through philosophical methods of inquiry. Historically, there has been a trend for philosophical systems to deal with work as an abstraction. Indeed, the major characteristic of philosophic inquiry is that it differs from ordinary reflective thought in that it is more abstract and utilizes concepts to formulate general principles and laws. Thus, in the early Christian centuries philosophy conceptualized work in terms of the prevailing idealism of the time. Later on during the Renaissance, work came to be viewed within a rationalistic framework of work as an idea. Then in the eighteenth century work became viewed in terms of the actual products of the work efforts via the philosophy of realism. More recently in the late nineteenth and twentieth centuries, the philosophical view of work is that of a changing value within an occupational hierarchy through the influence of experimentalism.

Educationally Oriented Sub-fields of Various Disciplines

Disciplines such as psychology, sociology, anthropology, and philosophy each have a sub-field which is primarily concerned with the educational implications and applications of the theory, research, and practice of that discipline. Although there are no theories of occupational choice or career development, per se, within these sub-fields, their areas of focus and the ideas which they utilize may further help the practitioner to perform his work in a more enlightened manner. Since it is beyond the scope of this monograph to describe all of the implications of the behavioral sciences for education in general and the guidance practitioner, several illustrative areas have been selected to suggest how these disciplines relate as a backdrop for the practice of counseling and guidance.

Educational Philosophy

A major contribution of educational philosophy has been to study the alternative viable goals of education and to identify the place of vocational preparation in the curriculum. Summarized in Table 1 are twelve major philosophies of education. Implicit in each of these philosophies is a somewhat different perspective on the nature of adequate occupational preparation in relation to the total educational endeavor. For example, a philosophy of education for intellectual discipline would view vocational education and occupational preparation as vulgar and inappropriate except in the form of the general training of the mental faculties which prepares the individual for many kinds of work. The philosophy of education for life adjustment, on the other hand, would stress a type of education which would prepare the individual for coping with life and its frustration, stress, and anxiety. In this philosophy, occupational preparation is explicit, but only one of many explicit foci. In the philosophy of education for national survival, on the other hand, the preparation for occupational choice and future work is an explicit educational concern and, indeed, is the major explicit effort in the educational process.

Educational Sociology

A major contribution of educational sociology has been to analyze and describe human relations in education. As potent a vehicle as psychology has been, it has given the field of counseling and guidance at best an incomplete insight or a partial perspective on the functioning of the school and the mission of counseling and guidance in that

TABLE 1

Basic Philosophies of Education

1. *Experimentalism:*	belief in an active school; emphasis on guided experience; learning solves present problems; knowledge and truth change; knowledge should not be revered just because it comes from the past; knowledge is derived from social experience.
2. *Classical Realism:*	stems from Plato and Aristotle; emphasis on the form of things; emphasis on general education and general laws; "theoretical"; stress on "big ideas."
3. *Education for Life Adjustment:*	purpose of education is to give youth attitudes and skills to cope with situations (problems) of everyday life.
4. *Education for Intellectual Discipline:*	emphasis on the "generative" subjects, training the mind, and basic learnings.
5. *Education for Psychological Maturity:*	goal is to help develop attitudes of self-understanding and self-acceptance.
6. *Education for Moral Character:*	function of education is to teach individuals the right thing to do; emphasis upon honesty, truthfulness, and industry.
7. *Protestant view of Education:*	religion and education shouldn't be separated; emphasis upon uniting Protestant ideas and the goal of education.
8. *Roman Catholic View of Education:*	general curriculum of the school is either viewed from a Catholic point of view or supplemented by religious instruction.
9. *Jewish View of Education:*	education is a continuing task which begins in the family and then goes out to the community; an ignorant individual can't be truly free; education is the "bread of life;" emphasis on intellectualism and tradition.
10. *A Conservative View of Education:*	goal of education is to transmit well-tested ideas and worthy traditions of the past; emphasis on the traditionalism and the cultural heritage.
11. *A Reconstructionist View of Education:*	society and culture oriented; curriculum of education centers on the problems of politics, religion, aesthetics, etc.

TABLE 1 (*Cont.*)

Basic Philosophies of Education

12. *Education for National Survival:*	education is an instrument of power; national survival depends upon proper uses of educational resources; emphasis upon proper allocation of human resources and talent.

setting. Hansen (1963) for example, has criticized counseling for being the monogamous mistress of psychology. It has been the primarily psychological orientation which has continued to limit the fundamental strategy of guidance to "cubicle counseling." While few theorists or practitioners would deny the centrality of counseling and individual appraisal techniques, a purely psychological orientation is a severely limited perspective. Teachers and administrators have been quick to point out the apparent insensitivity of counselors with the traditional psychological orientation to the broader social system of the school or other institution of which they are a part.

A sociological perspective suggests that the counselor should be cognizant of the social system in which he functions and sensitive to various aspects of that social system as he interacts with students, staff, and parents. Thus, Coleman (1959) has studied the social climates of a group of high schools and concluded that there is an adolescent society and that the adolescent society has values and goals which are different from those of the adult society. Several recent studies have investigated the nature of the social system of the school in terms of its impact on both students and teachers (Aubrey, 1967; Riester and Zucker, 1968). The influence of individual peers and peer groups upon the individual has also been well documented. While the organizational structure of the school, its social climate, and the structure and influence of its subsocieties do not have a direct bearing in offering a theory of occupational choice or vocational development per se, a sensitivity to the sociological perspective is useful for understanding the nature of the educational setting and its influence upon the behavior of students and staff.

A Historical-Religious Perspective on Work

In the long history of man prior to Christianity, work had been viewed as a necessity, a hardship, and a curse. From prehistoric time to the classical Greek period, the problem of sheer existence required man to expend a major amount of his energy to insure his own survival and to provide for a few minimal luxuries above the pure subsistence level. Religion was an integral part of the daily life in ancient Greece and Rome. The gods were seen as closely involved in the everyday life of man and often intervened in the day-to-day life of mortal men. Work was seen as a curse by the Greeks and Romans. In fact, the Greek word for work — *ponos* — and the Roman equivalent — *poena* — mean sorrow, fatigue, travail, burden, etc. Man was condemned to work by the gods. Slavery was introduced to allow citizens of Greece and Rome to pursue more worthwhile and pleasurable activities than the wearysome toil that was necessary to maintain the general level of civilization which had been attained by these countries. Slaves did the dreary physical work, thereby enabling the citizen to pursue the more worthy goals of life such as independence from external forces, self-sufficiency, and self-satisfaction. The life of the farmer, free tradesman, or craftsman, while more desirable than that of a slave, nevertheless did not enable the individual the opportunity of seeking truth and practicing virtue.

The contemporary Christian view of work is derived from the long tradition of the Hebrews. The Hebrews viewed work as a means for atoning for the original sin of man. Work is hard and necessary and represents a noble attempt by man to restore the fundamental God-man harmony that resulted from creation. The work of man and the work of God represent parallel efforts to develop the justice and happiness of the Kingdom of God on earth. Both intellectual contemplation and the manual labor of the common man are dignified and worthwhile in the Hebrew tradition.

Surprisingly, there is no major global and comprehensive formulation of the religious meaning of work in terms of the general process of guidance or the more limited processes of vocational counseling or the dissemination of occupational information. The Judeo-Christian tradition views vocational choice as a calling by God. In the Old Testament, for example, Abraham was the first person to be called by God. "By faith Abraham obeyed when he was called to go to a place which he was to receive as an inheritance; and he went out, not knowing where he was to go (Hebrews 11:8)." Commenting on this first "vocational choice," Smith (1963) notes: "As a people of God, Abraham and his kinsfolk were summoned out with a corporate vocation, which was the foundation for each person's calling (p. 18)." The New Testament tradition constitutes an extension of the concept of "God's calling." Jesus called men from a variety of occupations to be his disciples and when the small group of disciples became the nucleus of the Christian Church an even broader "calling" occurred. Writing to the Church (a "called" group) the Apostle Paul wrote: "I beg you to lead a life worthy of the calling to which you have been called (Ephesians 4:1)."

During the medieval period the prevailing religious view of work was that priests and monks had a calling (vocation) and that other people had jobs (occupations). Manual work was a necessity, even for certain members of religious orders, but manual work was of lower dignity than prayer and contemplation. Slowly, the Catholic Church, largely through the efforts of St. Thomas Aquinas, accepted lay work as essential and worthwhile. But work still constituted an acceptable means to an end rather than an activity which had intrinsic worth and dignity. Throughout the medieval period it was not life on earth that represented the major focus of the Christian, but rather life in the hereafter. The Protestant reformers, on the other hand, gave a new emphasis to work. Work in a secular context was seen by them as equal in worth to work done in a religious setting. For them, work came to be seen as essential — a way of carrying out God's purpose in an individual's life. Luther saw work explicitly as carrying out God's purpose. Only God's work, however, was good. Work could not be used as a means for accumulating wealth or for upward social mobility. Calvin's ideas about work represented the transition from the early Reformation thinking to modern Protestant religious thought in regard to the place of work in the life of the Christian. From Calvin's ideas summarized below there emerged the work ethic:

1. The purpose of man is to glorify God.
2. All men must work because it is the will of God.
3. The profit from work should not be enjoyed by man through the purchase of material belongings.
4. Wealth should be either reinvested into making more wealth or used to help establish the Kingdom of God on earth.
5. The individual should select a calling and pursue it as a religious duty.
6. Success (profit) indicates that the vocation chosen by the individual is pleasing to God.
7. Work not only can be, but must be used to increase one's upward mobility, for it is only through self advancement that the individual can best further the Kingdom of God.

The Golden Age of Work occurred in the nineteenth century. Work became universally accepted in Western civilization as the major source for society's progress. Essentially similar traditional views emerged from both Catholic and Protestant theologians. This point of view has been identified as Christian humanism (Moynihan, 1964). Essentially, Christian humanism holds that the ideal fully developed person is fully man and fully Christian. Jesus (God-man) is seen as the perfect model. Man is inherently good, capable of being elevated by grace, and is synthesized with the supernatural through Christian beliefs and virtuous living. Through work, man transforms the world, perfects it, humanizes it by integrating it into his own life and thereby works in order to complete God's creation. Work represents an expression of human personality seeking to discover and to unfold the image of God within himself. The other two basic expressions of human personality include man's relationship to God and his life as a marriage partner and parent. Christian humanism holds that all honest work is sacred. Thus, all workers who are Christian dedicate their work to God and use their career not only to earn a living but also to build a better (Christian) world.

A Literary Perspective on Work

Perhaps the most overlooked source of insight into the nature of vocational choice and work in general has been the field of literature. Both psychiatrists and psychologists note that various types of great artists have been penetrating interpreters of the human psyche and have offered incisive descriptions of personality and the dynamics of daily life. Freud, on the occasion of his seventieth birthday, disclaimed credit for discovering the unconscious, saying that the credit properly belongs to imaginative artists whom he called valuable allies "... whose testimony is to be rated high, for they usually know many things between heaven and earth that our academic wisdom does not even dream of (Shrodes, 1950, p. 38)." The breadth and depth of these literary insights about work are reflected in various kinds of literature. The following quotations include selections from novels, poems, short stories, plays, essays, the Bible, etc. (Bartlett, 1953)

1. Blessing and Nobility
   - A. William Blake (1757–1827) The busy bee has no time for sorrow.
   - B. Thomas Carlyle (1795–1881) All work . . . is noble; work is alone noble . . . A life of ease is not for any man, nor for any god.
   - C. Bishop Richard Cumberland (1632–1718) It is better to wear out than to rust out.
   - D. Thomas Dekker (1570–1641) Honest labour bears a lovely face.
   - E. Francois de Salignac de la Mothe Fenelon (1651–1715) By labor wisdom gives poignancy to pleasure, and by pleasure she restores vigor to labor.
   - F. Marcus Aurelius Antoninus (A.D. 121–180) In the morning, when thou art sluggish at rousing thee, let this thought be present: "I am rising to a man's work."
   - G. Sir William Osler (1849–1919) Though a little one, the master-word work looms large in meaning. It is the open sesame to every portal, the great equalizer in the world, the true philosopher's stone which transmutes all the base metal of humanity into gold.

H. Jean Jacques Rousseau (1712–1778) Temperance and industry are man's true remedies; work sharpens his appetite and temperance teaches him to control it.
I. Eugene Fitch Ware (1841–1911) Work brings its own relief; he who is most idle has most grief.
J. Booker Washington (1858–1915) No race can prosper till it learns that there is as much dignity in tilling a field as in writing a poem.

2. Curse
   A. Charles Dickens (1812–1870) My life is one demd horrid grind.
   B. Rudyard Kipling (1865–1936) More men are killed by overwork than the importance of the world justifies.
   C. Charles Lamb (1775–1834) Who first invented work and bound the free?
   D. Karl Marx (1818–1883) Constant labor of one uniform kind destroys the intensity and flow of a man's animal spirits, which find recreation and delight in mere change of activity.
   E. Silvia Townsend Warner (1893–)
      John Bird, a laborer, lies here,
      Who served the earth for sixty year
      With spade and mattock, drill and plough;
      But never found it kind till now.
   F. Sir William Watson (1858–1935)
      Too long, that some may rest,
      Tired millions toil unblessed.
   G. Bible: (Genesis III:19) In the sweat of thy face shalt thou eat bread.

3. Fitted to Man
   A. Kenyon Cox (1856–1919)
      Work thou for pleasure — paint, or sing, or carve
      The thing thou lovest, though the body starve —
      Who works for glory misses oft the goal;
      Who works for money coins his very soul.
      Work for the work's sake, then, and it may be
      That these things shall be added unto thee.
   B. Douglas Malloch (1877–1938)
      If you can't be a pine on the top of a hill,
      Be a scrub in the valley — but be
      The best little scrub by the side of the rill;
      Be a bush if you can't be a tree.
   C. Michal de Montaigne (1533–1592) Saturninus said, "Comrades, you have lost a good captain to make him an ill general."
   D. Publilius Syrus (Circa 42 B.C.) Everyone excels in something in which another fails.
   E. John Ruskin (1819–1900) In order that people may be happy in their work, these three things are needed: They must be for it: They must not do too much of it: And they must have a sense of success in it.

. . . .

When men are rightly occupied, their amusement grows out of their work, as colour-petals out of a fruitful flower.

F. William Shakespeare (1564–1616) The labour we delight in physics pain.

G. George Bernard Shaw (1856–1950) This is the true joy in life, the being used for a purpose recognized by yourself as a mighty one; the being thoroughly worn out before you are thrown on the scrap heap; the being a force of Nature instead of a feverish selfish little clod of ailments and grievances complaining that the world will not devote itself to making you happy.

H. Humbert Wolfe (1885–1940) If a man has a talent and cannot use it, he has failed. If he has a talent and uses only half of it, he has partly failed. If he has a talent and learns somehow to use the whole of it, he has gloriously succeeded, and won a satisfaction and a triumph few men ever know.

4. Fruits

A. Gertrude Franklin Atherton (1857–1948) No matter how hard a man may labour, some woman is always in the background of his mind. She is the one reward of virtue.

B. Miguel de Cervantes (1547–1616) Diligence is the mother of good fortune.

C. Euripides (484–406 B.C.) Toil, says the proverb, is the sire of fame.

D. Robert William Service (1874–). Not by my sins wilt thou judge me, but by the work of my hands.

5. Proletariat

A. Friedrich Engels (1820–1895) By bourgeoisie is meant the class of modern capitalists, owners of the means of social production and employers of wage-labor. By proletariat, the class of modern wage-laborers who, having no means of production of their own, are reduced to selling their labor-power in order to live.

B. Karl Marx (1818–1883) The proletarians have nothing to lose but their chains. They have a world to win. Workers of the world, unite!

6. Right to

A. Thomas Carlyle (1795–1881) "A fair day's-wages for a fair day's-work": it is a just demand of the governed men ever made of governing. It is the everlasting right of man.

7. Worker

A. Plato (427–347 B.C.) Under the influence of poverty or of wealth, workmen and their work as equally liable to degenerate.

B. William Shakespeare (1564–1616) The fashion of these times, where none will sweat but for promotion.

. . . .

I am a true labourer: I earn that I eat, get that I wear, owe no man hate, envy no man's happiness, glad of other men's good.

8. Weary Worker
   A. Edwin Markham (1852–1940)

      Bowed by the weight of centuries he leans
      Upon his hoe and gazes on the ground,
      The emptiness of ages in his face,
      And on his back the burden of the world.

9. Earning a Living
   A. Wilfred Wilson Gibson (1878–) All life moving to one measure — daily bread.
   B. Horace Greeley (1811–1872) The best business you can go into you will find on your father's farm or in his workshop. If you have no family or friends to aid you, and no prospect opened to you there, turn your face to the great West, and there build up a home and fortune.
   C. Karl Marx (1818–1883) From each according to his abilities, to each according to his needs.
   D. William Somerset Maugham (1874–) There is nothing so degrading as the constant anxiety about one's means of livelihood . . . Money is like a sixth sense without which you cannot make a complete use of the other five.
   E. Ogden Nash (1902–)

      O money, money, money, I am not necessarily one of those who think thee holy.
      But I often stop to wonder how
      thou canst go out so fast when thou comest in so slowly.

   F. William Shakespeare (1564–1616) O, how full of briers is this working-day world!
   G. William Temple (1881–1944) Human status ought not to depend upon the changing demands of the economic process.

Social Critics' Perspective on Work

There is a group of thoughtful and perceptive writers whom this author calls the social critics. In general they are insightful and practically theoretical in an attempt to expose social inconsistencies and injustices. Like other formulations described in this chapter their theorizing has not resulted in theories of occupational choice or career development. Rather, their efforts have been directed toward highlighting work (among other social phenomena) and its role in the general dehumanization, fragmentation, and hypocricy of contemporary American society. To date, the contribution of these writers' perspectives toward a theory of vocational choice has not been generally acknowledged. Nevertheless, their qualities of journalistic style, candor, incisiveness, etc., contribute a perspective which is missing from the more traditional and formal theories.

In *The Vanishing Adolescent* (1962) Friedenberg views adolescence as a period in which the individual must define himself, i.e., find out who he is and what he really feels. Self-definition occurs as the adolescent clarifies the meaning of his experience. Both the general culture and the school, however, in their emphasis upon cooperation and group adjustment impair this quest for identity. Material success and contentment become the life goals to be attained by social sensitivity and social integration. Thus, the process of becoming an American entails a fundamental renunciation of individuality, for individuals are a nuisance. Some other important goals of education are (a) the distribution of status to students who acquiesce to school demands and perform well, (b) formal instruction, and (c) compiling and maintaining a dossier (cumulative record) of each student's grades, personality, test scores, etc. In his search for selfhood the adolescent must make a rather continuous self-appraisal and derive adequate self-esteem from the self-appraisal. The school threatens self-esteem as the staff, the curriculum, and the co-curriculum distinctly favor a relatively small segment of the student population whose background attitudes, values, and general behavior are those of the lower-middle class.

Friedenberg (1962) further criticizes the school not only for its basic ungraciousness but also for the shallowness of its conception of dignity:

> To this ungraciousness of the school and the shallowness of its conception of dignity, I attribute its paradoxical failure to achieve among its students the norm of personality it prizes so highly. For personality conceived as a norm cannot be developed. A school that restricts freedom, invades privacy, and limits enterprise in order to promote normality is certainly not going to promote growth.

Thus, Friedenberg contends that the adolescent as we have known him is vanishing because the personal integration — the sense of identity — is disappearing. What Friedenberg did not foresee was the adolescent revolt in colleges and in high schools against the curriculum, teaching methods, rules, regulations, codes of dress and conduct, the draft, and policy making practices in both education and the broader culture.

Elsewhere, Friedenberg (1967) in *The Coming of Age in America* critically reviews the treatment of adolescents in contemporary high schools noting that secondary education has fallen very short of its high ideals of helping people understand the meaning of their lives, becoming more sensitive to the meaning of other people's lives, and relating more effectively with other people. He characterizes education as sentimental, extrinsically motivated, emotionally dishonest, distrustful, controlling, infantalizing, punishing, fragmenting the individual's experience, forestalling the development of good taste, conformity oriented, providing little support in the quest for identity and, in general, forcing youth to acquiesce to a dehumanizing controlling institution which views students as "colonials." The net results of the acquiescence is that youth are acculturated before they are truly old enough to resist. The school thereby becomes the gateway to "opportunity" as viewed by typical middle class values. Friedenberg also criticizes our society for its lack of provision of meaningful jobs for adolescents. While the traditional jobs of delivery, elevator operator, messenger, etc., may not have been very worthwhile, the disappearance of these jobs largely because of automation has left the adolescent with no legitimate role except that of a high school student. Ironically, he has no meaningful work but does get money from parents. Commenting on the vested interests of maintaining the (colonial) dependency of adolescents, Friedenberg (1967) notes:

> The school is interested in keeping him off the streets and in its custody. Labor is interested in keeping him off the labor market. Business and industry are interested in seeing that his tastes become fads and in selling him specialized junk that a more mature taste would reject . . . he cannot easily work out an entirely personal and responsible pattern of economic behavior because he has no serious economic status.

Later on in life,

> most people must expect to earn their living in jobs that permit no personal style, require no skill, and are often not worth doing. There is no way education can make such work meaningful, though education can deal with it liberally by scrutinizing the economic arrangements, and their underlying social and moral assumptions, that condemn people to do it (Friedenberg, 1967).

In *The Status Seekers* Vance Packard (1959) has looked at the rather well-known concept of social class and has written an insightful exposé of the neurotic role of status in contemporary life. He denounces the myth that technological advances and general prosperity have eliminated or even greatly reduced class differences. Packard believes that there are many pressures operating to make our society more rigid and caste-like. One by one he vividly describes the basically unhealthy influence of status seeking in such areas as (a) snob appeal in purchasing homes, (b) conspicuous consumption in items bought, (c) individual and group behavior in clubs, lodges, etc., (d) beliefs and behavior of various religious groups, (e) neurotic child-rearing practices, (f) political beliefs and behavior, and (g) sex appeal.

Two areas of inquiry in Packard's book are of particular relevance to vocational choice and career development. A general description of child rearing summarizes the general differences among various socio-economic groups in such areas as attitudes toward pregnancy of expectant mothers, leisure activities, parental discipline, peer relations, behavior in school, general attitudes and values, etc. Following a summary of the relative status of various occupations and occupational groups, Packard makes the following generalizations regarding the dynamics of our rewards system:

1. Among the professions, your best opportunity, moneywise, is to be a doctor.
2. Blue-collar skills are gaining on the lower white-collar skills in relative reward.
3. One white-collar skill that is highly rewarded is salesmanship.
4. The best way to assure oneself of a six-figure income is to be a business manager or owner.

Concluding that the reward system is out of kilter, he notes that businessmen and groups that control the flow of new talent into a field are over-rewarded while intellectual pursuits and jobs in non-profit organizations are under-rewarded. The following quotation summarizes his position: ". . . any reward system that year after year pays a wailing crooner approximately one hundred times as much as the Chief Justice of the United States Supreme Court is somewhat out of balance." Later in a summary of the "Pecking Orders in Corporate Barnyards" (Ch. 8) Packard notes that the social systems of many work organizations are becoming formalized and rigidified caste systems. Commenting in particular about business life he notes that the trappings of power, prestige, and privileges are often more important than the actual raise in salary. Thus, the major motivation and reward for work among some occupational groups become larger offices, better wall-to-wall carpeting, the movement from oak to walnut to mahogany desks, location of the office, etc.

Whyte's exposition on the life of the *Organization Man* (1957) describes in great detail the goals, the dynamics of corporate life, and the general life style of those middle class workers who have ". . . left home, spiritually as well as physically, to take the vows of organization life to be . . . the mind and soul of our great self-perpetuating institutions." The organization man type of worker performs an eufunctional role in the system by maintaining and promoting the goals of the system. He is the well-known stereotype of the suburbanite with all of its trappings. Riesman in *The Lonely Crowd* (1950) summarizes this type of worker and this style of living as other-directedness. He gets his cues for living and decision-making not from an inner core of values (inner directed), but from a super-social sensitivity to the expectations of other people whom he feels he should either impress or be in tune with or both. The female homologue of the organization man is a syndrome described by Betty Frieden as *The Feminine Mystique* (1963). The mystique is an unjust unfair myth which seeks to perpetuate, in effect, the position of the woman in the "organization" of the home. Describing "the problem that has no name," Frieden notes:

> The problem lay buried, unspoken, for many years in the minds of American women. It was a strange striving, a sense of dissatisfaction, a yearning that women suffered in the middle of the twentieth century in the United States. Each suburban wife struggled with it alone. As she made the beds, shopped for groceries, matched slipcover materials, ate peanut butter sandwiches with her children, chauffeured Cub Scouts and Brownies, lay beside her husband at night — she was afraid to ask even herself the silent question — "Is this all?"

Frieden documents the basic unhappiness of women who succumb to the feminine mystique and center their lives only on the home. Given this limited work role, women cannot begin to fulfill themselves. Frieden advocates that women must first get rid of the housewife image and plan lives as whole women. She believes that it is only through creative work that a woman can know herself as a person. Just finding a job is not enough. The job must be a challenge and offer a significant experience as part of a worthy life plan. The job must also allow her to grow as a vital contributing member of society.

In *Growing Up Absurd,* Goodman (1956) makes the same general critical observations about the quality of much of contemporary life as the above writers but focuses more directly on occupational choice and work. The following quotes convey the essence of Goodman's criticisms:

> It's hard to grow up when there isn't enough man's work . . . there get to be fewer jobs that are necessary or unquestionably useful; that require energy and draw on some of one's best capacities; and that can be done keeping one's honor and dignity.
>
> . . . workmen are indifferent to the job because of its intrinsic nature: it does not enlist worthwhile capacities, it is not "interesting"; it is not his, he is not "in" on it; the product is not really useful.
>
> But by and large our economic society is *not* geared for the cultivation of its young or the attainment of important goals that they can work toward. This is evident from the usual kind of vocational guidance which consists of measuring the boy and finding some place in the economy where he can be fitted; chopping him down to make him fit; or neglecting him if they can't find his slot.

An Economic Perspective on Work

The early rather informal theories of occupational choice had a fundamentally implicit view of man as "economic man." The primary motivation for work was seen to be economic and the process for achieving economically oriented goals was envisioned as primarily rational. Rather quickly, however, it became apparent that the "economic man" theory of occupational choice was inadequate. Writing of the economic perspective on occupational choice Samler (1961) notes:

> It is a one dimensional portrayal of man who, contrary to the soundest of folk wisdom, lives by bread alone. There is no question of the need for a common framework of economic considerations. . . But the skeleton, like all such structures, lacks individuality, character, and uniqueness.

Thus, the more recent theories have emphasized the psychological and sociological aspects of occupational choice and vocational development. But in the attempt to broaden the conceptual base for vocational psychology, the contribution of economic theory appears to have been largely overlooked except perhaps, by Super (1957). A theory is an abstraction or a caricature of reality, but not reality per se. Thus, it is possible for a practitioner to accept a theory which, while accurate in its basic formulation, is nevertheless incomplete and therefore less than an optimal guide for practice. It would appear that in their zeal to develop more adequate theories of occupational choice, many theorists have eliminated or overlooked the field of economics. Some potentially useful partial insights from economics include: (a) the role of economic motivation in occupational choice, (b) the dynamics by which manpower shortages and surpluses, welfare policies, traditions, unions and professional organizations, training costs, fluctuation in sex and age distributions among workers, mobility patterns, etc., effect the supply and demand of workers, (c) the impact of business cycles, national prosperity, tariff policies, cost of living and similar factors on the meaning and use of wages, (d) the direct and indirect influence of family income on socioeconomic status and the many related occupationally relevant phenomena, and (e) demographic data pertaining to wages and salaries among groups of people in various occupations.

Summary

Faced with the realities of rapid changes in the occupational structure and the general world of work, our society has increasingly relied upon guidance practitioners to aid youth in their occupational choices and career development. The almost overwhelming task of providing adequate help to youth through a broad gauged approach to guidance requires that the practitioner deal with a vast amount of data relating to both the individual and the world of work. Theory is useful because it enables the practitioner to order and to make sense out of the data. Moreover, theory provides the practitioner with some basic guidelines for practice. While traditional theories of occupational choice and vocational development will be presented in subsequent chapters, this chapter has surveyed formulations from related disciplines in an attempt to present the broad panorama of formulations which have emerged as theoreticians with various perspectives have grappled with the dynamics and meaning of work.

As noted above, the formulations described in this chapter may be characterized as fragmentary, segmental, of limited scope, and too ancillary to be of direct help to the practitioner. In varying degrees, depending upon the formulation, these limitations appear to be useful. The practitioner who is unaware of these formulations misses the background ideas regarding the process which he is attempting to guide or facilitate. The theories and other formulations in this and subsequent chapters thus constitute a guide and an aid in the practitioner's knowing first how the complex vocational behavior of man has been conceptualized and secondly, how he can bring to bear his own education, experience, and professional skill in fostering better vocational choices and/or more adequate career development.

The major implication of theory for the practitioner is that it can be a way of knowing and a general guide for practice. Attempts at theory building in the field of counseling and guidance are recent phenomena. Historically, the field has tended to be practice-centered rather than theory-centered. The immediate tasks of helping students and clients to lead fuller lives, avoid maladjustment, make good vocational decisions, etc., has taken precedence over the more long-term considerations of defining the parameters of ethical practice, analyzing the implications of prevailing practices, and building an adequate theoretical base for the work of the practitioner. The recent concerns over ethics and theory building in the areas of counseling and occupational choice reflect the growing maturity and sophistication of a field seeking admission to the family of mature professions.

Aside from the major considerations of occupational choice and career development which have been proposed largely within a psychological context, there have been several other frames of reference within which occupationally relevant behavior may be viewed. For the most part these "minor" theories of occupational choice have stemmed from the fields of anthropology, sociology, economics, literature and religion. Work has not escaped the scrutiny of contemporary social critics either. In general the formulations described above are not theories in the strict sense of the term. Rather they are theoretical speculations. Disarticulated and highly segmental, they lack the completeness and form requisite for an adequate basis for the work of the practitioner. Nevertheless there are many partial but valuable insights to be derived from these formulations.

2

Theories of Occupational Choice

The traditional way of conceptualizing human development in the area of work and work-related activities is best captured by the term occupational choice. Basically, the various theories of occupational choice described in this chapter hold that at a given point in time the individual makes the selection of an occupation. Although the theories differ widely regarding the dynamics of occupational choice, as a group they emphasize the choosing of an occupation as a relatively distinct event. Although a number of factors appear to influence occupational choice, each theory tends to emphasize certain factors and dynamics at the expense of others. The impact of theories of occupational choice upon the field of counseling and guidance is clear from the survey of these theories.

Trait and Factor Theory: Matching Persons and Jobs

The first well-articulated theory of occupational choice and the most durable one is derived from the psychology of individual differences. Specifically, it has been referred to in various ways: trait psychology, the psychology of individual differences, trait-measurement psychology, differential psychology, the actuarial or factorial approach to occupational choice, and the most popular term — trait and factor theory. Trait and factor theory evolved from the early pioneering work of Galton and Cattell, coupled with the later development of the testing or psychometric movement. One of the most succinct statements of the fundamental tenets of trait and factor theory is presented by Williamson (1965) who notes that the individual is organized in terms of a unique pattern of capabilities and potentialities (traits). These traits, in turn, are correlated with the requirements of different jobs. Thus, there is a rather homogeneous set of qualities (factors) which are both needed for success in each job and possessed by workers within any given job category. Testing, i.e., the objective measurement of traits, is the best means for predicting future job success. Each individual attempts to identify his own traits and to find a way of working and living which will enable him to use his capabilities effectively.

Katz (1963) summarizes the nature of trait and factor theory and its general implications for guidance as follows:

1. Each person is "keyed" to one or a few "correct" occupations.
2. If left alone, the individual would gravitate toward the right occupational choice.
3. Without assistance, however, wasted time and motion and some possibility of choosing the wrong occupation tend to occur.
4. The "key" can and should be learned during early adolescence.
5. The correct or appropriate occupation greatly influence educational decisions.
6. Both the occupational choice and subsidiary decisions should remain constant over a period of time.
7. In summary: the final occupational goal can be known early and should determine preliminary decisions related to and leading up to that goal.

The elements of trait and factor type theory are clearly evident in Parson's (1909) original description of occupational choice and the model of appropriate guidance for helping the individual with occupational choice. In simplified terms, trait and factor theory holds that (a) people have different traits, (b) each occupation requires a unique set of characteristics of its members, and (c) vocational guidance should match people and jobs. Parallel thought is evident in Parson's description of vocational guidance in the familiar three-step process of (a) studying the individual, (b) studying occupations, and (c) matching the right person with the right job. Similarly, the National Vocational Guidance Association (NVGA) (1937) names the study of the individual, the study of occupations, and counseling as the major components of vocational and educational guidance.

To date, this simplistic and pragmatic mode of thought has provided the essential framework for the application of the refined methods of psychometric assessment, the development and utilization of occupational information, and the use of various counseling systems. Although other theories have come into existence since the development of trait and factor theory, the trait and factor approach has continued to thrive and to exert a great deal of influence upon American thought regarding the nature of occupational choice and the helping relationship.

Need-Drive Theories: Occupational Choice as a Means for Satisfying Various Needs

The concept of motivation has held a central place in the field of psychology for a number of decades. Need-drive theories of motivation view the individual as having one, several or many needs. Needs, in turn, are transformed into a force (drive) which impels the person toward need-satisfying objects, persons, or activities. The motivation to satisfy needs may be either cognitive or conative (emotional); the motivation may be conscious or unconscious; the motivation may be expressed directly or indirectly. The individual's behavior which is directed toward satisfying his needs is typically envisioned as being goal-oriented. A number of theories have described work as a means for satisfying needs.

Some General Need Theories

Forer (1953) has proposed a rather general theory in which he describes occupational choice as being somewhat blind, impulsive, emotional, largely unconscious, and sometimes impractical. Although it constitutes an important factor, economic need and the economic motive is secondary. Often the individual simply does not know why he has selected a specific job. Occupational choice (or the lack of choice) is fundamentally a personal process, whereby the individual expresses his basic personality and satisfies his basic needs without being aware of why he is behaving the way he does. Schaffer (1953) studied the relationship between job satisfaction and need satisfaction and postulated that the most accurate prediction of general job-satisfaction can be inferred from the extent that the person's most important needs are met. He identified the following as job-oriented needs: recognition and approbation, affection and interpersonal relationships, mastery and achievement, dominance, social welfare, self-expression, socioeconomic status, moral value scheme, dependence, creativity and challenge, economic security, and independence. Individuals vary in their needs, and in general, the degree to which the person's two or three strongest needs are satisfied determines the extent of his general job satisfaction.

Although neither Maslow (1954) nor Allport, Vernon, and Lindzey (1951) have directed specific attention to occupational choice, per se, implicit in their formulations is the notion that success, satisfaction, adjustment, fullness of life, etc., are linked to the extent that the individual can satisfy a basic hierarchy of needs or value system needs. Maslow describes man's need structure in terms of a hierarchy in which lower order needs must be fulfilled before the high-order needs can be met. Maslow's hierarchy needs, summarized below, has been utilized as the basic motivational framework for a number of generalized considerations of human functioning such as mental health, general adjustment, classroom dynamics and marital behavior:

1. Physiological needs.
2. Safety needs.
3. Need to belong and to be loved.
4. Need for importance, respect, self-esteem, independence.
5. Need for information.
6. Need for understanding.
7. Need for beauty.
8. Need for self-actualization.

In like manner, Allport, Vernon, and Lindzey (1951) have devised an instrument which is based upon Spranger's (1928) value typology of types of men. They attempt to measure the relative prominence of six basic interests, motives (needs), or evaluative attitudes:

1. *Theoretical:* characterized by a dominant interest in the discovery of truth and by an empirical, rational, intellectual approach.
2. *Economic:* emphasizing useful and practical values; conforming closely to the prevailing stereotype of the average American businessman.
3. *Aesthetic:* placing the highest value on form and harmony; judging and enjoying each unique experience from the standpoint of its grace, symmetry, or fitness.
4. *Social:* emphasizing altruism and philanthropy.
5. *Political:* primarily interested in personal power, influence, and renown; not necessarily limited to the field of politics.
6. *Religious:* mystical, concerned with the unity of all experience and, seeking to comprehend the cosmos as a whole (Anastasi, 1959).

Presumably, for both Maslow and Allport, Vernon, and Lindzey, the individual makes his decisions, including his occupational choice, on the basis of his system of values (needs) and his general personality orientation.

Psychoanalytic Theory

The major contribution to a psychoanalytic interpretation of occupational choice has come from Brill (1949). The psychoanalytic conception of how an individual chooses an occupation rests upon the two key concepts of sublimation and identification. In the process of sublimation, socially unacceptable motives find expression, i.e., are changed in form (sublimated) into socially acceptable behavior. Occupations are chosen as general or specific sublimations of fundamental instinctual wishes or needs. Psychoanalytic theory emphasizes the familiar threefold character of the psyche — id, ego, and superego — with much of human behavior determined by unconscious motivation. Through work, the individual can release part of his psychological id energy in a transformed (sublimated) activity, for energy which would be directed to fulfilling such needs directly would often be unacceptable to society. The process of identification is also important, for the persons with whom the individual sympathetically relates or affiliates play a critical role and influence the direction taken in the act of sublimating an occupational choice.

Shown in the table below are various instinctual needs and occupations providing socially acceptable outlets for these needs. The examples of occupations have been selected from psychoanalytically oriented literature and research (Jones, 1923; Zilboorg, 1934; Drasgow, 1957).

Need or motivational pattern	Occupation
Sadomasochism	Surgeon or butcher
Voyeurism	Photographer
Domination	Teacher
Exhibition	Actor
Fascination of urination and water in general	Civil engineer who builds bridges
Concern with toilet training	Toilet fixture salesman

On the other hand, Hendrick (1943), also theorizing within a psychoanalytic frame of reference, feels that the sublimation/identification explanation of occupational choice is inadequate. He proposes a "work principle" derived from the "mastery instinct" in which man has a need to control, change, or develop his environment through intellectual and neurological processes. Thus, as the individual integrates his behavior and develops and applies skills related to work, he thereby satisfies his need emanating from the mastery instinct. Whereas the sublimation/identification theory emphasizes occupational choice as a means for fulfilling sublimated id needs, the mastery instinct/work principle theory stresses occupational choice and subsequent work behavior as an ego function.

Bordin et al. (1963) have developed the most systematic formulation of occupational choice within a psychoanalytic context by extending and delimiting the highly generalized formulations of other psychoanalytic writers. The strategy of Bordin and his associates was to select and study a small number of rather different occupations and through them to present the theoretical framework, methodology, and generalizations that would be appropriate for studying and understanding occupational choice within the broad spectrum of occupations. Plumbing, accounting, and social work were selected as representative occupations. Each occupation is then described in terms of its ability to satisfy needs along various psychic dimensions or body zones. The psychic dimensions of occupations include nurturing, oral, manipulative, sensual, anal, genital, and rhythmic needs. Each occupation has a different degree of involvement in and ability to satisfy these needs. Also, each occupation has a unique instrumental mode, i.e., a set of tools, techniques, or behaviors for satisfying each psychic dimension. The objects dealt with, e.g., money, needs of clients, pipes, etc., also vary from occupation to occupation. Work also has a sexual mode in that it may be a masculine, feminine, or nonsex-linked type of job. Lastly, there is an affective component to each occupation which may produce either an emotional experience, isolation, or a reaction formation.

Thus, the unique emphasis of psychoanalytic theories of occupational choice is upon the differential ability of various occupations to satisfy instinctual needs, to gratify impulses, and to reduce anxiety rather than emphasizing differential traits in people as requisites for success and satisfaction in various jobs. It was Brill and others who forged the general parameters of the theory. Hendricks represents the dissenting line of thought. Bordin and his associates have added new dimensions and specified the aspects of work which satisfy various needs. At best, however, the psychoanalytic theories of occupational choice are gross. It is assumed that the normal individual will experience little, if any, difficulty with occupational choice. Further, if occupational choice problems do occur, the psychoanalytic interpretation would be that the occupational problem is merely symptomatic and is therefore of secondary importance to causal factors which would lie in the realm of deeper psychological processes of unresolved conflicts, ego defense mechanisms, and similar dynamics.

Roe's Theory: The Influence of Early Parent-Child Relationships

Anne Roe has evolved a theory of occupational choice which has certain psychoanalytic qualities but is clearly broader in scope than the psychoanalytic interpretations described above. Roe's theory has evolved from three basically different lines of research. One area of theory building has focused upon the classification of occupations (Roe, 1956). After analyzing the available classification systems, she devised a new taxonomy consisting of eight groups of occupations (service, business contact, organization, technology, outdoor, science, general culture, and arts and entertainment). In addition to the eight broad occupational groups, she further subdivided each group into eight levels. Later, she reduced the number of levels to six. Thus, her final formulation consists of an 8 x 6 arrangement of cells into which every occupation can be placed. Shown below is an example of some levels of jobs in the organization occupational group.

Occupational Group: Organization

Level	General category	Sample occupations (service)
1	Professional and managerial (1)	Personal therapist, counselor
2	Professional and managerial (2)	Social worker, probation and truant officer
3	Semiprofessional and small business	YMCA official, detective, police sergeant, welfare worker
4	Skilled	Barber, chef, practical nurse, policeman
5	Semiskilled	Taxi driver, waiter, city fireman
6	Unskilled	Chambermaid, hospital attendant, elevator operator, watchman

In a second line of research, Roe investigated the developmental backgrounds and personalities of various types of research scientists (Roe, 1951a; Roe, 1951b; Roe, 1953). Two major findings emerged from these studies. First, there are clear-cut major personality differences between physical-biological scientists and social scientists. Second, child rearing practices appear to influence at least in part the personality differences between these two groups of scientists. These first two lines of research provide the groundwork for the eventual development of a theory of occupational choice. Her classification system provides the essential framework for describing the occupational structure. The studies of scientists provide clues to the fundamental dynamics of occupational choice.

The third line of research has sought to develop a theory to explain the psychological differences among workers in the various groups and levels of the classification system. Roe's major assumptions and hypotheses stem from the studies of scientists, coupled with a utilization of Maslow's hierarchy of need paradigm described above. Roe has articulated Maslow's general motivational theory with certain assumptions about the influence of early parent-child relationships to form the basis of her theory of occupational choice. Specifically, she postulates that there are three basically different psychological climates as a function of early parent-child relations (Roe, 1957):

1. Emotional concentration on the child.
   a. Overprotecting climate: the major focus of the parent-child relationship is on the parent satisfying and overprotecting the child. The child's basic low-order needs are quickly gratified, but the higher order needs are gratified only when the child complies with parental (social) expectations. This syndrome in childhood leads to a basic pattern in later life of becoming dependent upon others and generalized conforming behavior.
   b. Overdemanding climate: the overdemanding parent-child climate is similar to the overprotective climate in many ways. A basic difference between them, however, is that the overdemanding parent emphasizes achievement as interpreted by the parent.
2. Avoidance of the child.
   a. Neglecting climate: in this type of parent-child relationship the parent avoids the child and his responsibility to the child. Little effort is directed toward satisfying the child's needs.
   b. Rejecting climate: the basic pattern of the rejecting parent-child relationship is one in which the parent actively ignores the well being of the child. The rejection may involve the neglecting of physical and/or psychological needs.
3. Acceptance of the child
   a. Casual climate: in this type of home climate the child is accepted by the parent but the parent-child relationship is a loose and very informal one.
   b. Loving climate: like the casual parent-child relationship, provision is made for gratifying the child's needs at all levels. Children of both casual and loving accepting home climates tend to seek gratification of needs at all levels.

The two most important dimensions of an occupation, i.e., occupational group and occupational level, constitute the basis for classifying occupations. The occupational group chosen is determined by the type of early parent-child relationship. There is a direct causal relationship between the type of parent-child climate and the development of the individual's need hierarchy. Thus, warm parent-child relations, e.g., accepting (accepting and casual) and overprotecting, result in the child learning to satisfy his needs largely through interaction with other people. Later when he selects an occupation, he therefore chooses person-oriented occupations, e.g., service occupations. Conversely, individuals who experience cold early modes of childrearing, e.g., avoidance (neglecting and rejecting) and overdemanding climates, learn to satisfy their needs through avenues not involving people. In their occupational choices, these individuals typically select occupations involving objects (e.g., technology), animals (e.g., outdoor), or ideas (e.g., science). Within each occupational group there are six levels of occupations. The level selected within any given occupational group is influenced by the person's need intensity. Need intensity, in turn, is composed of such elements as constitutional (genetic) factors and the involuntary (unconscious) basic pattern of expending psychic energy to satisfy needs and is limited by such factors as intelligence and socioeconomic background.

In summary it is the basic parental attitude toward the child rather than specific childrearing techniques, per se, which shape the child's need structure and pattern for satisfying his needs. Once developed and utilized for meeting needs in general, the fundamental mode of need satisfaction influences occupational choice, for occupations come to be viewed as a means for satisfying needs. Both the organization and the intensity of the individual's needs drive him toward certain occupations and occupational goals. Early parent-child experiences and the resultant pattern of need satisfaction dynamics thus constitute the two cornerstones of Anne Roe's theory, for they determine the individual's moving toward person-oriented occupations or nonperson-oriented occupations.

Hoppock's Theory: A Composite View

Hoppock feels that it will take an extended period of time to generate enough research evidence to confirm or contradict existing theories, let alone adequately test theories being developed and those not yet devised. He asserts that the absence of ideal formulations, coupled with the presence of many reasonable theories suggests a strategy of evolving a composite theory. Hoppock notes that what he has developed is a series of speculations rather than a comprehensive set of neat hypotheses. Although the theory is stated in the form of postulates with a focus upon occupational choice as a means for satisfying needs, a variety of factors influence occupational choice. Values, participation in an occupation, association with people in various occupations, educational experiences, psychological factors such as unconscious motivation and, lastly, broad economic, sociological and cultural factors constitute some other significant determinants of occupational choice.

Drawing from several existing theories, Hoppock (1967) summarizes his theory as follows:

1. Occupations are chosen to meet needs.
2. The occupation that we choose is the one that we believe will best meet the needs that most concern us.
3. Needs may be intellectually perceived, or they may be only vaguely felt as attractions which draw us in certain directions. In either case, they may influence choices.
4. Occupational choice begins when we first become aware that an occupation can help to meet our needs.
5. Occupational choice improves as we become better able to anticipate how well a prospective occupation will meet our needs. Our capacity thus to anticipate depends upon our knowledge of ourselves, our knowledge of occupations, and our ability to think clearly.
6. Information about ourselves affects occupational choice by helping us to recognize what we want and by helping us to anticipate whether or not we will be successful in collecting what the contemplated occupation offers to us.
7. Information about occupations affects occupational choice by helping us to discover the occupations that may meet our needs and by helping us to anticipate how well satisfied we may hope to be in one occupation as compared with another.
8. Job satisfaction depends upon the extent to which the job that we hold meets the needs that we feel it should meet. The degree of satisfaction is determined by the ratio between what we have and what we want.
9. Satisfaction can result from a job which meets our needs today, or from a job which promises to meet them in the future.
10. Occupational choice is always subject to change when we believe that a change will better meet our needs.

Summary

The common element among all of the above theories of occupational choice is that each person chooses an occupation at some given point in his or her life. The central focus of these theories is upon the process of choosing an occupation, the factors influencing the choice, and the adequacy of the choice as measured by need satisfaction, success, or personal adjustment. Presumably if a good occupational choice is made, the individual finds happiness and advancement and remains in that occupation. Inadequate choice leads to unfulfilled needs, failure, or maladjustment. In the latter case, the resultant frustration and tension create the need for another occupational choice — hopefully a better choice. There is little, if any, cognizance taken of occupational choice and work in the total life span of the individual. Each job is dealt with separately and relatively independently from preceding or subsequent choices.

3

Theories of Vocational Development

The pervasive theme running throughout the various theories of occupational choice is that one, several, or a cluster of dynamic factors operate upon or within the individual and that at some point in his life each individual chooses an occupation either in conjunction with these dynamic forces or as a response to them. Each person is viewed as being better suited for one job than all of the others. Hopefully, he can guide himself toward finding that one best job and can accordingly make that appropriate occupational choice. Counseling and guidance are important at the major decision point at which an occupation is actually selected. If the individual chooses the correct occupation then he becomes happy, satisfied, successful, well adjusted, socialized, etc. Since the converse is also true, then if he selects the wrong occupation he must have remedial assistance. For each of the theories described above there is the implicit notion that the individual must find a correct "slot." Historically, the correlative assumptions relating to the best kind of help for the individual in his search for the correct occupational choice has led to (a) an emphasis upon crisis guidance at critical choice points, (b) the placement of guidance services almost exclusively in the secondary school, (c) a reliance upon an almost certain need for remedial assistance because of initially wrong choices, and (d) the utilization of subsequent remedial services within a variety of non-school community agencies.

There is another group of theories, however, which views the occupational life of the individual from a very different point of view. These theories view the individual from a developmental perspective. Each person is seen proceeding through a number of different periods, phases, or life stages. Vocational development is one aspect of the many-facetted development of the individual. Basically, the individual does not choose an occupation, but rather makes a series of occupational and occupationally-related choices at different life stages which, when taken cumulatively, result in vocational development rather than an occupational choice, per se. Occupational choice does not occur at a given point in life; vocational development emerges over a long period of time as the individual pursues vocational and vocationally-related goals. People are not keyed to "a correct occupation;" each person is capable of being successful and satisfied at many jobs. The adequacy of a person's work life is not determined by the quality of a single occupational choice; it is defined by the total life style, including the work style, that he develops. Practitioners should not help people only at the "choice point;" people need help over long periods of time. Because this latter group of theories emphasizes looking at the individual over a long period of time and because they emphasize stages of vocational development, these theories have come to be known as developmental theories. The related strategies for helping individuals with their vocational development have emerged as developmental guidance and developmental counseling.

As in the case of most scientific investigation, research and theory building in the area of vocational development could not emerge until the necessary *Zeitgeist* (prevailing feeling or spirit of the time) had been developed. Thus, there were a number of historical antecedents to the actual emergence of theories of vocational development. Perhaps the most important general area of inquiry required before fruitful theories of vocational development could emerge was the field of developmental psychology. More specifically, theory building in the area of personality development and advances in the conceptualization of mental health and treatment of mental illness prepared the way for a readiness among theoreticians to begin the task of building theories of vocational development from a developmental point of view.

Historical Antecedents to Contemporary Theories of Vocational Development

In the field of psychology it was Terman (1925) who in his classical study of the concomitants of superior intelligence provided the first hint of a developmental approach to work and work-related activities. Terman studied the educational, marital, and vocational adjustment of intellectually superior people. His use of a cross-sectional approach in which he studied samples of people of different age groups had a somewhat developmental quality, but lacked the detail necessary for a theory of vocational development, per se. Later, Lazersfeld (1931) studied the general growth of occupational thinking. Perhaps the most significant breakthrough came from the work of Buehler (1933). Investigating the development of psychological life stages, Buehler identified the following general periods of life: (a) growth stage (birth to age 15), (b) exploratory stage (age 15–25), (c) establishment stage (age 25–45), (d) maintenance stage (age 45–65), and (e) the decline stage (age 65–death). At about the same time, several pioneering sociologists were beginning to study occupational behavior from their own vantage point (Davidson and Anderson, 1937; Bell, 1938, 1940). Carter (1940, 1944a, b) worked in the area of vocational choice and aspiration and concluded that these problem areas were developmental in quality rather than static as implied by trait and factor theory. Shortly thereafter, Bordin (1943) proposed a dynamic (developmental) theory concerning the emergence of vocational interests and just one year before that Super (1942) began a line of research that has continued to the present time.

A later group of studies added more form and substance to the emerging developmental interpretation of vocational behavior. Hollingshead's (1949) classical investigation entitled *Elmstown's Youth* utilized a case study method to identify the influence of status on educational and occupational opportunity and the development of the individual during the school years and into the early work years. Friend and Haggard (1949) also used case histories to study the relationship between occupational adjustment and family background. Erikson (1950) and Havighurst (1950) proposed unique but fundamentally similar formulations regarding the general course of human development and the role of psychosocial crises (Erikson) and developmental tasks (Havighurst) in the developmental process. The basic outline of their formulations has been summarized as follows:

1. Individual growth and development is continuous.
2. Individual growth can be divided into periods of life stages for descriptive purposes.
3. Individuals in each life stage can be characterized by certain general characteristics that they have in common.
4. Most individuals in a given culture pass through similar developmental stages.
5. The society makes certain demands upon individuals.

6. These demands are relatively uniform for all members of the society.
7. The demands differ from stage to stage as the individual goes through the developmental process.
8. Developmental crises occur when the individual perceives the demand to alter his present behavior and master new learnings.
9. In meeting and mastering developmental crises, the individual moves from one developmental stage of maturity to another developmental stage of maturity.
10. The task appears in its purest form at one stage.
11. Preparation for meeting the developmental crises or developmental tasks occurs in the life stage prior to the stage in which it must be mastered.
12. The developmental task or crisis may arise again during a later phase in somewhat different form.
13. The crisis or task must be mastered before the individual can successfully move on to a subsequent developmental stage.
14. Meeting the crisis successfully by learning the required task leads to societal approval, happiness, and success with later crises and their correlative tasks.
15. Failing in meeting a task or crisis leads to disapproval by society (Zaccaria, 1965).

Coupled with the proposals noted above, Erikson and Havighurst provided the overarching concepts of psychosocial crises and developmental tasks together with a generalized framework of human development from which the more specialized theories of vocational development could be derived. Havighurst (1953, 1956) first expanded his original formulation of developmental tasks by elaborating upon the general sociological, psychological, and biological dynamics of developmental tasks together with a further specification of the tasks themselves and how they are typically mastered. Thus, Havighurst defined a developmental task as

> . . . a task which arises at or about a certain period in the life of the individual, successful achievement of which leads to happiness and success with later tasks, while failure leads to unhappiness in the individual, disapproval by society and difficulty with later tasks (Havighurst, 1953).

One of the developmental tasks of the adolescent period, for example, is that of selecting and preparing for an occupation. The other developmental tasks of adolescence include the following:

1. Accepting one's physique.
2. Accepting a masculine or feminine role.
3. Forming new relations with age-mates of both sexes.

4. Attaining emotional independence of parents and other adults.
5. Achieving assurance of economic independence.
6. Developing intellectual skills and concepts necessary for civic competence.
7. Desiring and achieving socially responsible behavior.
8. Preparing for marriage and family.
9. Building conscious values in harmony with an adequate scientific world-picture.

Although the developmental task concept had gained rather wide acceptance in a variety of fields such as education, child rearing, and counseling and guidance, the formulation continued to have a very generalized focus until Havighurst specified the concept of developmental tasks in terms of a six stage schema of vocational development. The schema synthesizes the concepts of vocational life stages, psychosocial crises, and vocational developmental tasks (Havighurst, 1964). In the schema there are six stages of vocational development. In the first stage (ages 5–10) the individual identifies with a worker, e.g., mother, father or other significant person, and thus the concept of working becomes an integral aspect of the ego ideal. Then (ages 10–15) the person must acquire the basic habits of industry. The third stage (ages 15–25) consists of the individual acquiring identity as a worker in the occupational structure as he chooses, prepares for, and gets initial work experiences. During the next stage (ages 25–40) the individual must become a productive person through mastering the fundamental skills of his occupation and becoming occupationally upwardly mobile. Gradually (ages 40–70) the emphasis shifts as the individual successively (a) focuses his attention away from himself and more toward societal responsibilities, (b) views himself as a responsible citizen in a productive society, (c) rises to the peak of his occupational career and (d) begins to work at inducting youth and younger adults into the occupational structure. In the last stages (ages 70-death) the individual contemplates his life and whether or not it has been productive and socially responsible.

Thus, Havighurst's general concept of developmental tasks identifies the foci for crisis in human development. As the individual meets and masters the critical developmental tasks, he proceeds from one life stage to another. The above schema specifies the course of vocational development and the tasks related to the general developmental task of selecting and preparing for an occupation. As the individual is confronted by vocational developmental tasks and reacts to them, a general life style and a work style emerges whereby he becomes (a) a maintainer of society who contributes to the society through work that does not hold a central place in his life, (b) an ego-involved entrepreneur of society whose work both contributes to the welfare of society and constitutes an anchor-point of meaning in the person's life, or (c) one of the alienated who is uncommitted to work and at best a fringe member of society (Havighurst, 1964). This major life theme that emerges as the individual encounters developmental tasks and develops an attitude toward life and society defines the role of work and its meaning in the life of the individual.

Ginzberg's Theory: An Approach to a General Theory

Ginzberg, Ginsburg, Axelrod, and Herma (1951) surveyed existing theories, found them inadequate, and then sought to develop and partially test a theory — or what they called an approach to or an approximation of a theory. Ginzberg's theory was the first one that was explicitly developmental and specifically a theory of occupational choice. Obviously, at the time Ginzberg was developing his theory, the distinction between occupational choice and vocational development had not yet been made. Ginzberg used a cross-sectional sampling method to study a carefully selected group of individuals who he felt had maximum freedom in choosing an occupation. He selected children of upper middle class parents. To further insure the fact that the sample would have real freedom of choice each member of the sample had to be male, Protestant or Catholic, of Anglo-Saxon origin, and living in an urban setting. He then interviewed his sample ranging from sixth grade to graduate school concerning their vocational choices. Simply stated, the study found that (a) occupational choice is a long-term process, (b) the process becomes increasingly irreversible, (c) the eventual choice represents a compromise between what the individual would ideally prefer and the available realistic possibilities, and (d) that the entire process occurs in a series of rather definitive stages or periods.

During the fantasy period (childhood) there is a gradual change in focus from occupational choices in the early part of the period reflecting a purely play-orientation to an approximate work-orientation at the end of the period. The fantasy thinking of this stage is reflected in the fact that children take no cognizance of reality, their own potentials and abilities, or the perspective of time. The play activities of childhood and the fantasy thinking of the first period, however, give way to the tentative period (early adolescence) in which reality factors e.g. interests, capacities, and values, time variables, work requirements, work rewards, etc., begin to influence decisions. Finally, in the realistic stage (middle adolescence) the individual explores, crystallizes a general occupational choice, and specifies an actual occupational choice within the psychological framework of realistic thinking.

Because the individual must resolve the basic conflict between his subjective desires and the pervasively objective limitations of the sociocultural milieu of which he is a part, the process of choosing an occupation is a compromise. Also, with each succeeding occupationally relevant decision many potential occupational choices are eliminated. Therefore, over an extended period of time the range of viable alternatives diminishes. With the passage of time, pressures of reality and defensive behavior relating to the expenditure of time, money, and energy limit the lines of access to many occupations. Furthermore, the individual can never return to the chronological and psychological point at which former decisions were made. Thus, occupational choice is irreversible in the very special sense of the term as described above.

Biological, psychological, and environmental factors may influence the course of occupational choice and constitute sources of variability among individuals' timing of occupationally relevant decisions. Other factors that influence the developmental process of occupational choice include reality testing experiences, identification with suitable role models, and the extent to which the individual is either work-oriented or pleasure-oriented. Thus, the sequence and timing of the various occupational choice stages are influenced by a variety of factors. The truly developmental quality of Ginzberg's theory is clearly evident from the fact that vocational choice is seen as a process, that the process is systematic, that it is predictable, and that occupational choice culminates in an eventual decision to enter a specific occupation. Obviously, the quality of that eventual choice reflects the course of development through the fantasy, tentative, and realistic periods, and influences the adequacy with which the individual will make future choices and implement these choices.

Holland's Theory:
A Theory of Personality and Model Environments

John Holland's theory (1959, 1966) represents an attempt to develop a theory which, while it is implicitly developmental, emphasizes the determinants of occupational choice. The major outlines of the theory are reflected in the following quotation:

> Essentially, the present theory assumes that at the time of vocational choice the person is the product of the interaction of his particular heredity with a variety of cultural and personal forces including peers, parents and significant adults, his social class, American culture, and the physical environment. Out of this experience the person develops a hierarchy of habitual or preferred methods for dealing with environmental tasks . . . The person making a vocational choice in a sense

> "searches" for [work] situations which satisfy his hierarchy of adjustive orientations. (Holland, 1959)

Holland proposes the construct of occupational environments which constitute the categories of stereotyped work settings. Occupational environments are used as a framework for organizing and classifying knowledge about occupational choice. The occupational environments (climates) also serve as a framework for predicting occupational choice, for Holland feels that at present it is more advantageous to predict general categories of occupational choice rather than specific occupations. When individuals choose an occupation, they have developed in varying degrees a developmental hierarchy, i.e., a hierarchy of preferred ways of coping with environmental tasks. This developmental hierarchy is composed of a ranking of modal personal orientations (typical coping styles) which are parallel to the occupational environments. For each occupational environment there is a corresponding modal personal orientation. In choosing an occupation the individual seeks an occupational environment which will enable him to cope with environmental work tasks in harmony with his major modal personal orientation.

In addition to a developmental hierarchy, Holland proposes the construct of a level hierarchy. The level hierarchy denotes the general occupational level toward which the individual gravitates. The level of occupational choice is influenced by the person's intelligence level and his self evaluation in terms of an apparently arbitrary four level categorization of the occupational structure. The occupational environments and modal personal orientations of Holland's theory along with representative occupations are summarized in Table 2.

Holland's theory postulates that the individual's growth and development are influenced by both hereditary and environmental factors. Specifics regarding the nature of these influencing factors and the dynamics involved are omitted. Presumably, through some type of learning process the individual develops habitual preferences (modal personal orientations) as he reacts to environmental demands. One of these environmental demands is that each person should make an occupational choice. Thus, faced with the task of choosing an occupation, he deals with this situation as with other situations. He seeks an occupational group as he is influenced by his stereotype of the various occupational groups comprising the world of work. His stereotypy of the occupational structure (occupational environments) may result in either a well defined or an ambiguous hierarchy. If the individual has a well-defined hierarchy and a strong preference for one type of occupational environment, then presumably, with adequate help such as occupational information and counseling, an easily made and stable occupational choice

PERSONALITY TYPES* (Modal Personal Orientation)		ENVIRONMENTAL MODELS* (Occupational Environments)	
Type	*Description*	*Type*	*Typical Occupations*
Realistic (Motoric)	Enjoys activities requiring physical strength; aggressive; good motor organization; lacks verbal and interpersonal skills; prefers concrete to abstract problems; unsociable; etc.	Realistic (Motoric)	Laborers, machine operators, aviators, farmers, truck drivers, carpenters, etc.
Intellectual	Task oriented, "thinks through" problems; attempts to organize and understand the world; enjoys ambiguous work tasks and intraceptive activities; abstract orientation; etc.	Intellectual	Physicist, anthropologist, chemist, mathematician, biologist, etc.
Social (Supportive)	Prefers teaching or therapeutic roles; likes a safe setting; possess verbal and interpersonal skills; socially oriented; accepting of feminine impulses; etc.	Social (Supportive)	Clinical psychologist, counselor, foreign missionary, teacher, etc.
Conventional (Conforming)	Performs structured verbal and numerical activities and subordinate roles; achieve goals through conformity.	Conventional (Conforming)	Cashier, statistician, bookkeeper, administrative assistant, post office clerk, etc.
Enterprising (Persuasive)	Prefers verbal skills in situations which provide opportunities for dominating, selling, or leading others.	Enterprising (Persuasive)	Car salesman, auctioneer, politician, master of ceremonies, buyer, etc.
Artistic (Esthetic)	Prefers indirect personal relationships, prefers dealing with environmental problems through self-expression in artistic media.	Artistic (Esthetic)	Poet, novelist, musician, sculptor, playwright, composer, stage director, etc.

*Terms within parentheses denote earlier nomenclature.

TABLE 2

A Summary of Holland's (1959, 1966) Personality Types and Environmental Models

can occur. An ambiguous or ill-defined hierarchy in which there are either several competing occupational environment preferences or else no preferred occupational environment in turn results in vacillation, indecision, or no choice. If the preferred occupational choice in the developmental hierarchy is blocked, then the individual will move to the second choice of occupational environment if there is one. In the event that there is no clear-cut preference or if several lower order preferences are of equal strength, vacillation or no choice occurs. The amount of and the accuracy of the individual's self knowledge and occupational knowledge are of critical importance in the process of occupational choice. Both self knowledge and occupational knowledge contribute to the understanding of the range, levels, and adequacy of potential occupational choices.

Tiedeman's Theory: The Process of Occupational Decision-Making and Adjustment

Tiedeman (1961) and Tiedeman and O'Hara (1963) propose a unique theory of vocational development in response to a need for an explicit formulation of the process of decision-making within the broader framework of career development. Erikson's (1950, 1959) theory of general personality development is utilized as the underlying theory of human development. Erikson outlines the process of personality, growth in terms of a construct that he calls the eight stages of man, the eight psychosocial crises of life, or the major components of the healthy personality. Within a general framework similar to that of Havighurst's (1950, 1953, 1956) developmental tasks, Erikson describes the individual growing and developing as he implements his biological potentialities within the social environment of family and community life. Thus, at each developmental stage the individual must face a major psychosocial crisis. It is in the resolution of these crises that the person develops from one developmental stage to another. Summarized in Table 3 are the psychosocial tasks and the consequences of not adequately mastering them.

General psychosocial crises have relevant counterparts in the special area of career development. The concept of career becomes a key part of the theory and a major aspect of career development is ego-identity. The pivotal position of ego-identity is evident in the following quotation:

> Ego-identity is the accumulating meaning one forges about himself as he wrestles with his meeting with society. It is the crystallizing premises of existence which one forges . . . in order to establish one's self in the world. Career development includes the development of an

TABLE 3

A Summary of Erikson's (1950, 1959) Psychosocial Crises

Life Stage	Psychosocial crisis	Description of Task	Result of Failure
Infancy	Gaining a sense of trust	Becoming trustful that basic needs will be met	Distrust
Early childhood	Gaining a sense of autonomy	Learning that he has an individual existence and his own power to decide	Shame and doubt
Middle childhood	Gaining a sense of initiative	Learning to initiate activities	Guilt
Late childhood	Gaining a sense of industry	Acquiring skills, basic physical, mental, and emotional activities	Inferiority
Adolescence	Gaining a sense of identity	Learning who one is	Role diffusion
Early adulthood	Gaining a sense of intimacy	Leading a healthy and satisfied sex life	Distantiation The repudiation, isolation, and if necessary the destruction of forces and people who are perceived as dangerous to the individual's existence
Middle adulthood	Gaining a sense of generativity	Helping to establish and guide the next generation	Stagnation
Late adulthood	Gaining a sense of ego-integrity	Feeling that one's life has been orderly, patterned, whole, etc.	Despair

orientation toward work that evolves within the psychosocial process of forming an ego-identity. (Tiedeman and O'Hara, 1963)

In essence, therefore, career development becomes the resolution of such fundamentally ego-relevant questions as "Who am I (at work)," "What shall I become (at work)," and "How will I implement my being (at work)," etc. Differentiation and integration are two important aspects of identity formation and career development in general. Through differentiation the individual identifies, studies, and evaluates various ideas, feelings, attributes, occupations, etc. Any given differentiation or distinction becomes relevant for the decision-making process, however, only as it articulates with other differentiations or distinctions. Thus, when a good articulation is made between various differentiations, synthesis or integration occurs. Differentiation and integration may occur in a variety of ways. A rational, i.e., reasoned and planned, process represents the highest and most desirable way for career-related decisions to occur. It is at this juncture that Tiedeman and O'Hara have made their major contribution, for they have proposed a rather complex model or paradigm of the decision-making process together with a description of how this process occurs. Their paradigm is presented in simplified form in Figure 1.

In essence, Tiedeman and O'Hara conceptualize career development unfolding as the individual resolves a group of (a) general psychosocial crises, (b) occupationally related special aspects of general psychosocial crisis, and (c) a life-long series of problems or decisions. Each problem-solving task involves a series of decisions and each decision is composed of the sub-stages specified in the paradigm under the two general aspects of anticipation or preoccupation and implementation or adjustment. For any one of the many career-related decisions that the individual must make in the course of career development the process of decision-making proceeds as follows: The individual begins the anticipatory or preoccupation stage by first experiencing a career-relevant problem. The problem may be an immediate problem such as that of an eighth grade boy who experiences the immediate problem of planning a program of courses for high school (grades 9–12) or it may be an anticipated problem as in the case of a person who knows that someday he will have to choose a first job. A decision must be made and a course of action must be eventually implemented. The two aspects of career development, i.e., decision and action provide the basic framework for the constructs of differentiation (anticipation and preoccupation) and integration (implementation and adjustment).

During the anticipatory stage of decision-making, the individual first carries out exploration. The person may, for example, focus upon alternative goals. Thinking at this point is typically very transitory, highly imaginary, fantasy oriented, and perhaps disarticulated. In terms of career development the individual mentally focuses upon such factors as premises, people, activities, objects, etc. involved in future behavior, and the possible effects of various courses of action. In effect, the individual is attempting to project himself into each of the alternative goals and courses of action he has begun to differentiate. In the crystallization phase or sub-stage the person makes a tentative choice after thinking and exploration have become stabilized. Often a number of partial crystallizations, further explorations and recrystallizations

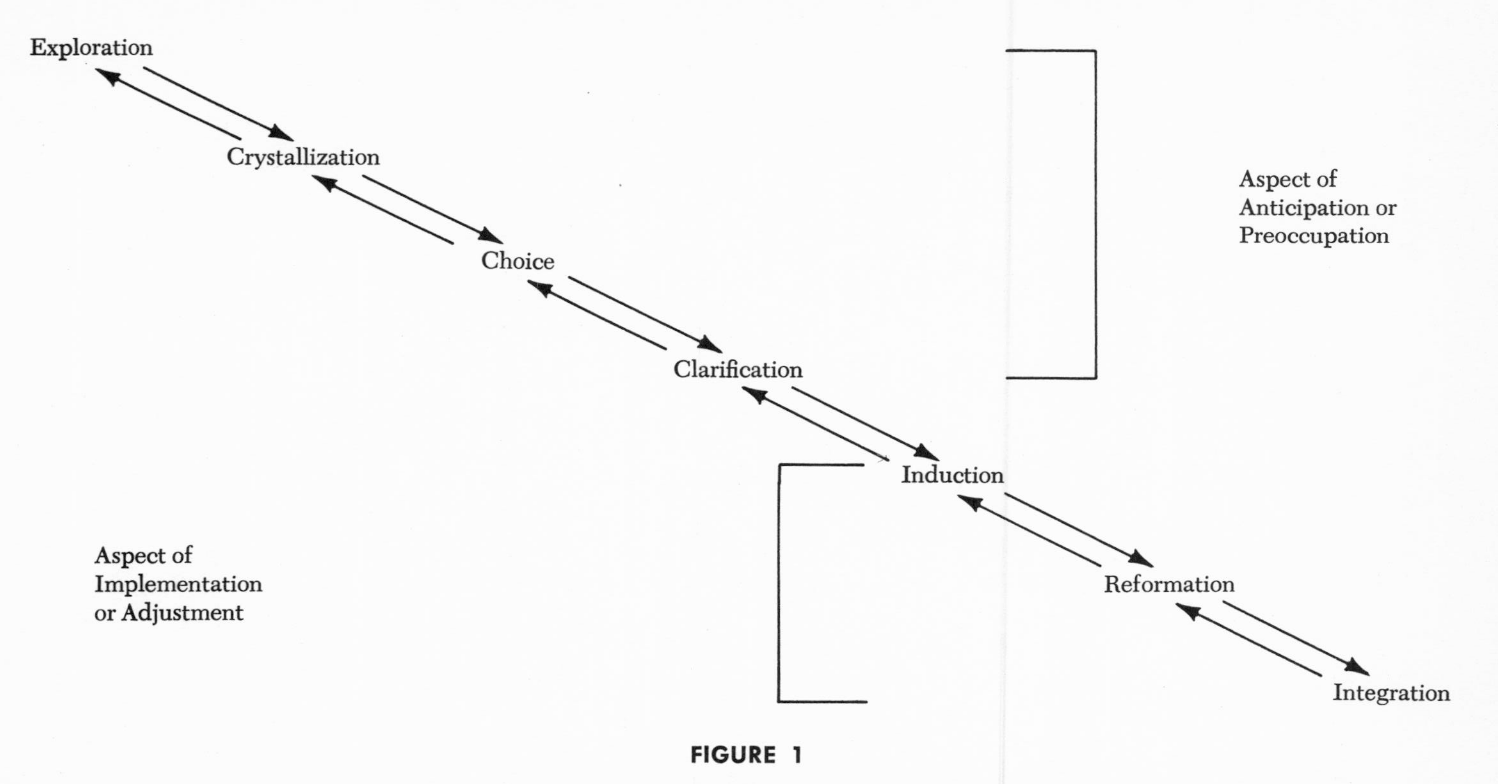

FIGURE 1

A Summary of Tiedeman's (1961) Paradigm: The Processes of Differentiation and Integration in Problem Solving

occur. With the final crystallization comes an actual choice of a particular goal, related activities, and the contemplation of the initiation of goal-oriented behavior. Clarification occurs next in which the future career-related behavior is elaborated upon, analyzed, and perfected. With the making of an actual decision and its clarification, the anticipatory or preoccupational stage ends and the individual proceeds to the next major stage, that of implementation or adjustment.

Induction occurs as the individual actually begins the implementing experience following choice and clarification. This sub-stage involves becoming recognized as a person, being generally defensive about one's self, and giving up an aspect of self for the general group purpose. As the individual continues interacting with others, discrepancies typically occur between the initial expectation and the realities experienced during the induction sub-stage. Reformation occurs when the person begins to assert himself and his ideas. The individual's goal at this point is to influence the relevant activities and the thinking of others in an attempt to adopt goals and activities in accordance with his own wishes. Whether the individual is in school or at work, varying degrees of success may result. Eventually, the person either achieves the changes he has sought or else he adjusts to the environment (work or school) through adaptation or withdrawal. If he leaves that setting, e.g., drops out of high school or college, then he must make a new decision. This new decision projects the individual into a new exploration→crystallization→choice→clarification→induction→reformation→integration sequence. Eventually some type of adaptation or integration occurs. Temporarily, at least, stabilization of thought occurs, the individual begins to commit himself to some course of action, and he feels happy and satisfied.

At this point the individual views himself and is generally viewed by others as being satisfied and/or successful. This contented equilibrium is eventually altered by one or a combination of such factors as psychological changes within the individual, co-workers, work setting, economic conditions, environmental tasks, etc. The person then senses a disequilibrium, i.e., a problem. A new decision must be made. New behaviors must eventually be implemented. The process of career development further unfolds as the individual copes with the decision-making and implementary or adjustment tasks. A series of problems are met; decisions are made; courses of action are followed; the individual proceeds from one developmental stage to another. Career development, i.e., successive differentiations and integrations may occur in chronological order, with some overlapping, or simultaneously.

As ego-identity emerges it assumes an increasingly more central influence on how the individual perceives himself, the general sociocultural environment, and his relationship to the world of work. More so than any other theorist, Tiedeman (1963) focuses upon how human activity is directed within the context of time. Thus, at each developmental stage an individual's time is pre-empted by biological factors, expectations for independence, and the search for identity, etc. Not only does the individual spend differing amounts of time on given activities or tasks at various developmental stages, but he must also contend with the time staging of various roles, e.g., person, child, friend, worker, spouse, parent, citizen, etc., associated with identity formation. Furthermore, the course of career development is characterized by continuities as the individual moves from one developmental stage to another and by discontinuities such as the interruption of career development by the requirement of service in the armed forces. Finally, Tiedeman explores the origins of occupational choice and the factors which predict occupational choice.

Tiedeman and his associates have made two major contributions to the field of vocational development theory. In keeping with their own theory they have integrated Erikson's general formulation of psychosocial crises with a viable theory of vocational development. Certainly, the resulting synthesis has enriched the thinking concerning the course of career development as it has been viewed against the broader backdrop of a widely accepted view of general human development. Secondly, they have further differentiated the process of vocational development through their specification of the etiology of occupational choice, the identification and ranking of factors influencing occupational choice, the focus upon the pre-emptive effects of various familial and societal expectations, the time staging of roles associated with achieving environmental tasks, and the elaboration of the nature of and dynamics involved in identity formation as it leads to the continuities and discontinuities of career development.

Super's Theory: Self-Concept Theory and Career Patterns

Super's theory of vocational development has evolved over a period of several decades, revealing the influence of three major bodies of thought. From the field of developmental psychology he has synthesized other formulations and has added new constructs of his own to propose a comprehensive general theory of vocational development. From the field of differential psychology he has drawn a different interpretation of the data than the earlier theories which had been focusing upon occupational choice. The cutting edge of Super's theory, however, has continued to be phenomenology (self-concept theory). Although the genesis of the basically developmental framework is evident in Super's early writing (1942), it was Ginzberg's (1951) theory that provided the impetus for generating further research which led to the formulation of Super's theory. Following Ginzberg's study, Super embarked upon a longitudinal study (1957), a series of theoretical works (1951, 1953, 1954, 1957, 1960, 1963, 1964) and a series of correlative studies conducted by his associates and students (Raylesberg, 1949; Lo Cascio, 1964; Bingham, 1966; Starishevsky, 1967). The basic framework of Super's theory consists of the developmental stages through which the individual passes in his career development. This framework synthesizes the formulations of Buehler (1933), Miller and Form (1949, 1951), and Ginzberg et al. (1951). Shown in Table 4 is a summary of the developmental stages of Super's theory.

TABLE 4

Stages of Vocational Development in Super's (1957) Theory

1. Growth Stage (Birth to 14 years):	A period of general physical and mental growth.
A. Prevocational Substage (Birth to 3):	No interest or concern with vocations or vocational choice.
B. Fantasy Substage (4–10):	Fantasy is basis of vocational thinking.
C. Interest Substage (11–12):	Vocational thought is based on the individual's likes and dislikes.
D. Capacity Substage (13–14):	Ability becomes the basis for vocational thought.
2. Exploration Stage (15 to 24 years):	General exploration of work.
A. Tentative Substage (15–17):	Needs, interests, capacities, values, and opportunities become bases for tentative occupational decisions.
B. Transition Substage (18–21):	Reality increasingly becomes a basis for vocational thought and action.
C. Trial Substage (22–24):	First trial job is entered after the individual has made an initial vocational commitment.
3. Establishment Stage (25 to 44 yrs):	The individual seeks to enter a permanent occupation.
A. Trial (25–30):	A period of some occupational changes due to unsatisfactory choices.
B. Stabilization (31–44):	A period of stable work in a given occupational field.

TABLE 4 (Cont.)

Stages of Vocational Development in Super's (1957) Theory

4. Maintenance Stage (45 to 65 years):	Continuation in one's chosen occupation.
5. Decline Stage (65 years to death):	
A. Deceleration (65–70):	A period of declining vocational activity.
B. Retirement (71 on):	A cessation of vocational activity.

Having proposed a general framework within which vocational development could be described, there remained the task of describing the specific course of that development. The concept of career pattern has been utilized as the conceptual vehicle for summarizing the grouping of major vocational events in the life of the individual. Taken together, the chronological series of vocationally-relevant events can be summarized and classified into a characteristic career pattern. Thus, while all individuals proceed through the same general developmental stages, individuals vary with respect to the type, sequence, and duration of various work and work-related activities. The various types of career patterns that can emerge are summarized below:

1. Male career patterns

A. Stable career pattern: School→A stable job for the remainder of the individual's working life.

B. Conventional career pattern: School→One or more trial jobs →Stable employment.

C. Unstable career pattern: School→Alternative sequence of trial and stable jobs with no permanent job or occupation.

D. Multiple trial career pattern: School→A series of trial jobs without any kind of work constituting a sufficiently prolonged or dominant type of employment to establish a career.

2. Female career patterns

A. Stable homemaking career pattern: School→Marriage with no significant work experience.

B. Conventional career pattern: School→Relatively brief work experience→Marriage.

C. Stable working career pattern: School→Stable job for remainder of work life.

D. Double-track career pattern: School→Work (optional)→A double career of simultaneous homemaking and work.

E. Interrupted career pattern: School→Some work experience (optional)→Marriage and child rearing→Return to the labor force.

F. Unstable career pattern: School→Any sequence of work, marriage, work, child rearing, work, etc., usually resulting from economic pressure (no stable work or homemaking experience).

G. Multiple trial career pattern: School→A series of unrelated trial jobs resulting in no genuine vocation.

With the formulation of developmental stages for a backdrop and with the concept of career pattern as a more specific description of the general style of the individual, the theory must specify the unique aspects of each person's vocational development. Phenomenology and self-concept theory constitute the theoretical frame of reference within which the unique experience of each person is interpreted. Within the more generalized framework described above, Super describes vocational development as the developing and implementing of a self-concept in the context of the world of work. The self-concept evolves and develops during the growth and exploratory stages. Through various types of general activities and exploratory behavior, the individual both differentiates himself from others and sees certain similarities between himself and others. As sensations, perceptions, and experience become more ordered and well articulated, the early self-percepts become broader, more abstract and comprehensive until the self concept, per se, emerges.

A vocational self-concept is a part of the global self-concept. It is the self-concept which guides the individual into and through his career experience. The further specification of self-concept development has occurred in terms of general self-concept development, the operationalization of self-concept theory and the translation of the general self-concept in vocational terms (Super, 1963). Rejecting the concept of occupational choice in favor of career development, Super consistently emphasizes the developmental process unfolding as the individual develops, specifies, and implements his vocational self-concept. The series of jobs a person holds represents a life-long search for a means of expressing himself in the world of work. People work to provide a livelihood, to maintain satisfactory human relations (e.g., recognition as a person, independence, self-expression, status, etc.), and to enjoy the satisfaction from working, per se. Work thus becomes a way of life, a means for satisfying needs, and a vehicle for achieving selfhood. A way of life is developed, needs are satisfied, and selfhood is achieved only in the arena of daily living. In recent years Super and his associates have turned to the concept of developmental tasks to provide the developmental framework for integrating (a) self-concept development, (b) the general dynamics of vocational development, and (c) the specific foci which dot the course of an individual's unique career pattern.

Super notes that the wholesome or psychologically healthy process of vocational development is a dynamic synthesis rather than a compromise as had been suggested by other writers. The synthesis is a result of the interaction of personal needs and resources of the individual and the economic and social demands of the culture. Societal demands act on most individuals through patterning of socialization. Developmental tasks represent these externally imposed learnings. Super notes, however, that as the individual matures, he tends to internalize some of society's expectations, e.g., developmental tasks, and thereby becomes more self-directive as he begins to develop goals for himself. Thereafter, developmental tasks may be considered to be self imposed. Thus, differentiation, integration and the development of independence characterize the meeting of developmental tasks. Super (1957) first refined Havighurst's general developmental task concept by specifying in more detail the nature of vocational developmental tasks. He identified a number of rather definitive tasks for each developmental stage. The vocational developmental tasks for the high school adolescent, for example, include (a) further development of abilities and talents, (b) choice of high school or work, (c) choice of high school curriculum, and (d) development of independence. The vocational developmental tasks of the young adult, on the other hand, are (a) choice of college or work, (b) choice of college curriculum, (c) choice of suitable job, and (d) development of skills on the job.

More recently, Super (1963) has approached vocational developmental tasks from a different perspective. Abandoning the earlier strategy of defining rather specific tasks, he has proposed a global and general formulation. In so doing he changed his basic approach from describing relatively discrete tasks similar to those of Havighurst to a much more compact and abstract formulation similar to that of Erikson. The vocational developmental tasks of Super's theory are summarized in Table 5.

TABLE 5

A Summary of Super's Vocational Developmental Tasks

Life Stage	Ages	Vocational Developmental Tasks
Early adolescence	14–18	Crystallizing a vocational preference
Middle adolescence	18–21	Specifying a vocational preference
Late Adolescence	21–25	Implementing a vocational preference
Young Adulthood	25–30	Stabilizing in a vocation
Middle Adulthood	30–50	Consolidating status and advancing in a vocation

Super's theory is perhaps the broadest and most widely accepted of the contemporary theories of vocational development. It has been systematically derived through the integration of the relevant aspects of existing theories and the unique additional contributions of Super and his associates. Unlike many other theories of occupational choice and vocational development, it has evolved rather slowly. Furthermore, the theory has been undergoing almost constant revision. During each of its own "developmental stages" Super's theory has been subjected to systematic research. Although it has been supplemented by research in the form of independent study by isolated investigators and by research through doctoral dissertations, the major continuing vehicle for research has been the twenty-year longitudinal Career Pattern Study. The data gathered from the group of ninth grade boys at the inception of the study have provided a more adequate understanding of the general course of vocational development as well as continuous testing of the essential elements of Super's career pattern theory.

Summary

The consideration of the various theories in this chapter completes the presentation of the theories of occupational choice and vocational development. Although the theories of occupational choice have continued to thrive, in recent years the theories of vocational development have constituted the main stream of thought and research in American vocational psychology. As the theories of vocational development have been extended and subjected to additional research, elements of non-psychological behavioral sciences have begun to be included as increasingly more integral aspects of these theories. In true developmental style, the vocational development theories emphasize the longitudinal quality of man's growth and development. Vocational development is seen as one aspect of the individual's total development. The unfolding of the individual's vocational development is seen as relatively continuous and long term, but divided into stages or life periods for purposes of description and presentation. As in the case of the formulations of occupational choice, the theories of vocational development acknowledge a wide range of factors which determine or at least influence the process of human development. The developmental quality of the latter group of theories reflects the growing general interest in human development and the correlative concern for understanding the etiology of human problems and maladjustment in order that they may be either eliminated or diminished in intensity through developmental (preventive) strategies.

4

Summary, Critique, Application, and Prospectus

A major theme in this monograph is that theories of occupational choice and vocational development are useful for the field of counseling and guidance by aiding in creating new knowledge, helping to achieve new syntheses of existing knowledge, providing a base for designing and/or strengthening existing preparatory programs, assisting in the development of new policies and practices, and guiding the work of the practitioner. The following quotation reflects the writer's point of view. "Theories without practices like maps without routes may be empty, but practices without theories like routes without maps are blind (Getzels, 1960, p. 42)." Having summarized the various theories of occupational choice and vocational development in prior chapters, the remainder of the monograph is devoted to the evaluation of these theories and the suggestion of the implications for practice of several representative theories.

Theory may be evaluated in two general ways. The first procedure is the objective approach which utilizes an objectively based methodology to evaluate theory against certain predetermined criteria. An external frame of reference is used to ascertain the extent to which a given theory meets the selected set of criteria of a good theory. Among the various formulations of the qualities of an adequate theory is that of Stefflre (1965) who notes that a theory must be (a) clear (high agreement among general principles), (b) communicable (easily understood), (c) comprehensive (possess enough scope to account for much behavior), (d) explicit (precise in that concepts can be checked against referents in the real world), (e) parsimonious (does not over-explain phenomena), and (f) that it generates useful research. Osipow (1968) evaluates theory in terms of its formal adequacy, explanatory adequacy, empirical support, generality, parsimony, operational adequacy, and logical consistency. Patterson (1966) feels that an adequate theory must have a set of stated assumptions or postulates. Furthermore, these assumptions or postulates must be related to each other; they must be internally consistent, and the relationships must be specified. Hypotheses, in turn, can then be derived from the statement of assumptions, definitions, and/or postulates. Essentially, the hypotheses are predictions of what should be found if the theory is valid. An adequate theory not only predicts new facts and new relations but also organizes and integrates what is known into some type of meaningful framework or frame of reference. Theory building is a continuous process of formulation, testing the formulation through hypotheses derived from the formulation, modifying the theory in light of the testing of hypotheses, reconstructing or adapting the theory, further testing, etc.

Carkhuff and his associates (1967) recognize both inductive and deductive functions of theory and outline the essential process by which adequate theory emerges:

1. Raw data are collected.
2. Facts and laws are derived from the data.
3. A theory is extrapolated from the facts and laws.
4. Theorems and/or hypotheses are derived from theories.
5. Research efforts result in the collection of additional raw data which may or may not support the theory.
6. Improved facts and laws emerge.
7. Improved theory is developed.
8. The above sequence occurs again and again and with each step the theory becomes more adequate.

The interested reader is referred to Borow (1964), Carkhuff, et al. (1967), Osipow (1968), and Super (1968a, b) for detailed evaluations of individual vocational theories against specific sets of criteria. If one agrees with Hemple and Oppenheim (1953) that there is a continuum among theories from those which describe to those which explain, then the adequacy of description and explanation represent two additional criteria for evaluating contemporary theories of occupational choice. In general, it appears that the type of theoretical content in the area of occupational choice and vocational development is similar to that in sociology, where Merton (1957) notes one group of sociological theorists who,

> seek above all to generalize, to find their way as rapidly as possible to the formulation of sociological laws. Tending to assess the significance of sociological work in terms of scope rather than the demonstrability of generalizations, they eschew the 'triviality' of detailed, small-scale observation and seek the grandeur of global summaries. At the other extreme stands a hardy band who do not hunt too closely the implications of their research but who remain confident and assured that what they report is so. . . . For the first group the identifying motto would at times seem to be: 'We do not know whether what we say is true, but it is at least significant'. And for the radical empiricist the motto may read: 'This is demonstrably so, but we cannot indicate its significance.

The vocational development theories of Super, Havighurst, Miller and Form, and Holland would appear to be comparable to the first group described in Merton's quotation, while trait and factor theory and the mass of demographic and correlational studies would be comparable to the second group in Merton's quotation.

It appears that if one attempts to evaluate contemporary theories of occupational choice and vocational development against rigorous criteria of formally adequate theories, i.e., against the standards of an ideal theory, then certainly all of the current theories are inadequate. There is general consensus, for example, that an ideal theory not only describes phenomena but also explains their occurrence. Many individuals who favor the theoretical models of the physical and natural sciences further stipulate that ideal theories reduce phenomena to measurable dimensions. Contemporary formulations fall far short of this lofty ideal. Realistically, the major shortcoming of contemporary formulations of occupational choice and vocational development appears to lie in a lack of systematic format development. Thus, when viewed within the perspective of absolute formal adequacy, contemporary theories of occupational choice and vocational development are at best emerging formulations or embryonic approaches to theory. Furthermore, significant changes would be necessary in order for contemporary formulations to be developed into more adequate content and scope as per the typical sets of objective criteria.

The subjective approach to theory assessment does not evaluate the worth of a theory against objective criteria. Rather, the general procedure consists of the practitioner beginning to understand himself and his own goals. Self-understanding or self-knowledge, in turn, provides an internal frame of reference for viewing his sociocultural environment, the work setting, and his role and function in that setting. In effect, the practitioner can utilize his own frame of reference as a point of departure for selecting personal and professional goals from the alternative goals available to him. After having selected relevant goals, the practitioner can then adopt and utilize appropriate means for achieving his goals. As a professional, he operates from a theoretical base interpreted within the context of pragmatic realities. The practitioner's functioning, i.e., his practices, are means or techniques for achieving his goals. The integral relationship among goals, means, theory, and practice is shown in Figure 2.

After establishing a set of goals, the practitioner can then select appropriate means for achieving these goals. The various source fields constitute the place to which the practitioner can look to find the per-

FIGURE 2

A Paradigm: The Derivation of Educational Practice from Integrated Theory

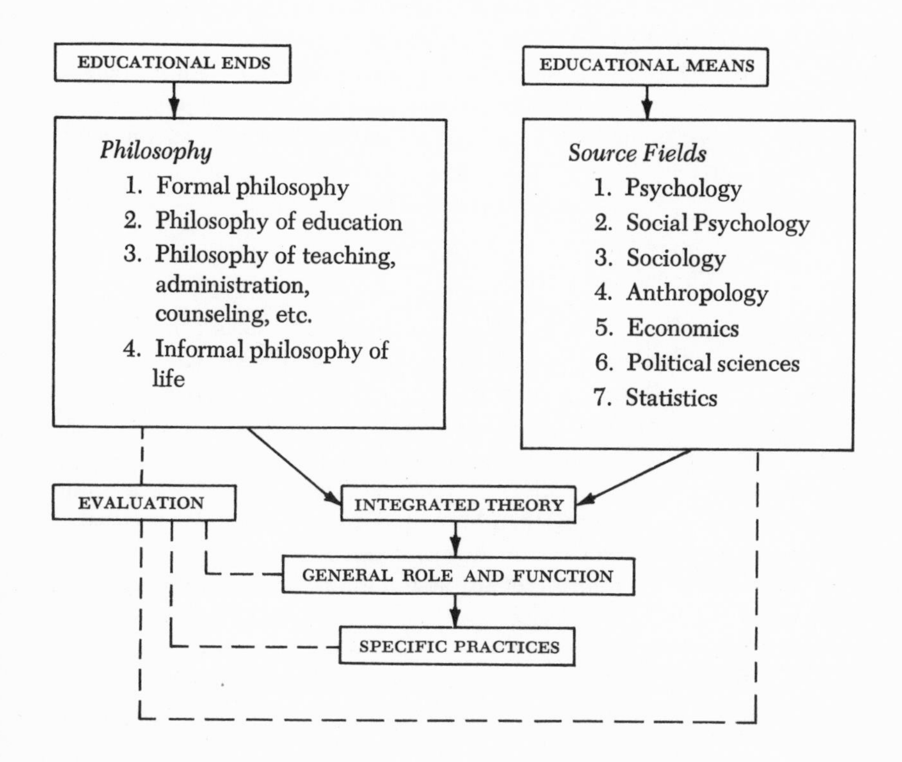

spectives, attitudes, frames of reference, theories, and skills which when mated with a set of goals constitute an adequate theoretical base for practice. A theoretical stance (integrated theory) thus contains elements of both objectives and appropriate techniques for achieving these objectives. As shown in Figure 2, the practitioner's general role and function can then be systematically derived from theory. Specific practices, in turn, can stem from the general role and function.

Theories of occupational choice and vocational development vary somewhat in their conception of the nature and dynamics of adequate vocational activities. Fundamentally, however, all of the theories envision the individual achieving success and happiness through work. The motivation of the prospective worker and his vocationally relevant behavior has been conceptualized in such terms as his being driven by instincts, satisfying needs, implementing a self-concept, mastering environmental tasks, earning money for an adequate standard of living, etc. Virtually all descriptions of the field of guidance include the notion that it should be concerned with vocational guidance. Thus, the utilization of a subjective approach to the evaluation and use of theory unfolds from the practitioner's understanding of himself, his own goals, and alternate goals of education and guidance. Formal philosophical systems, philosophies of education, and philosophies of guidance represent the relevant source fields for developing the ends, i.e., the goals of guidance. Thus, formal knowledge can be interpreted and evaluated in light of the practitioner's own informal philosophy of life and his personal goals. Some major goals of education and goals of guidance are shown on page 61.

Some Practical Applications of Occupational Choice and Vocational Development Theories

Regardless of whether or not the practitioner chooses to evaluate contemporary theories of occupational choice and vocational development from an objective or a subjective vantage point, if he decides to derive his vocational guidance practices at least in part from a systematic theoretical base, then he must decide upon how he will use a theory or a group of theories. If the practitioner elects a purist approach to theory selection, then he will select the single theory that is best for him and his work as he views it. He would then systematically derive his practice from the goals, assumptions, scope, and content of that theory.

Many practitioners, on the other hand, prefer to borrow elements of different theories and base their practice on the eclectic use of a number of compatible theories. In this multitheoretical or multidisciplinary

Goals of Education (Butts, 1955)	**Goals of Guidance (Cribbin, 1955)**
1. Character and moral development.	1. To develop student initiative, responsibility, self-direction, and self-guidance.
2. Mental discipline.	2. To develop in each student the ability to choose his goals wisely.
3. Literacy and information.	3. To know one's self, to know the school, and to be known by the school.
4. Vocational and practical aims.	4. To anticipate, avoid, and prevent crises from arising in the life of the student.
5. Civic or social aims.	5. To help the student adjust satisfactorily to school and life.
6. Individual devlopment.	6. To help the student recognize, understand, meet, and solve his problems.
	7. To assist the student in making wise choices, plans, and interpretations at critical points in his life.
	8. To help the student acquire insights and techniques necessary for enabling him to solve his own future problems.
	9. To assist teachers to teach more effectively.
	10. To help administrators and to foster the efficient administration of the school.
	11. To develop citizens who will participate in and contribute to the democratic way of life.
	12. Miscellaneous objectives: assisting in the home, helping the community, building ethical character, fostering human relations and developing international understanding.

approach, the practitioner would shift his theoretical focus. Sometimes he would view the individual from one vocational frame of reference and sometimes he would view the person from the vantage point of another occupational choice or vocational development theory. Similarly, the practices used would vary as the practitioner shifted from one theoretical stance to another.

A third possibility besides the purist (single theory or single discipline) and the eclectic (multitheory or multidisciplinary) approach is the synthetic (interdisciplinary) approach. In many ways the synthetic approach for using theory is the most complex and the most difficult to use in that it requires the various theories be meaningfully related and smoothly articulated with each other in terms of general content and implications for practice. The result of a synthetic theory is an amalgamation of a number of individual theories into hybrid formulation.

Described below are some practical applications of some representative theories from a purist perspective. Some implications of each theory for vocational guidance are briefly summarized. A practitioner wishing to develop some type of eclectic formulation could utilize elements of a very large number of possible combinations and permutations of the numerous theories described in this monograph in evolving his own eclectic theory of occupational choice or vocational development. Lastly, an example of a synthetic theory of vocational development is briefly described in terms of how such a theory could be made operational. Elements of phenomenology, self-concept, career pattern theory, psychosocial crisis theory, developmental task theory, vocational developmental task theory, developmental counseling theory, and developmental guidance theory are fused into a synthetic theory of developmental vocational guidance. Some specific vocational guidance practices in elementary schools, junior high schools and senior high schools will be outlined in an attempt to indicate how practice can flow from synthetic theory.

Trait and Factor Theory

The fundamental notion of trait and factor theory is that (a) people have trait characteristics such as attitudes, values, interests, aptitudes, etc., (b) jobs require differential factors for success, and (c) practitioners should match people and jobs. The major goal of trait and factor guidance is to assist students through helping them to make better choices. The major processes include individual work with students, group work, testing, educational and occupational information, and counseling. For each individual, the process of guidance unfolds in the familiar pattern of (a) helping him to know his own traits through the use of psychometric devices (tests, inventories, rating forms, case history [case study], etc.), (b) providing objective and verified information about the world of work, and then (c) through counseling, helping the individual to measure himself through a relatively cognitive process against the known requirements of school learnings and requirements of occupations. Brammer and Shostrum (1963) describe the educational-vocational model of counseling, and while the model is not linked directly with any particular vocational theory, the unmistakable imprint of trait and factor theory is quite clear:

(1) Establishment of the relationship.
(2) Statement and elaboration of the problem(s).
(3) General structuring of the nature of the counseling process.
(4) Discussion of the problem and collection of data (via interview, case history, tests, inventories, checklists).
(5) Individual appraisal (if tests are utilized).
(6) Occupational and educational study by the client.
(7) Discussion of data from the appraisal and from the client's individual study.
(8) Synthesis of the data into a meaningful plan.
(9) Discussion of steps necessary to carry out the plan.
(10) Follow-up procedures including possible reassessment and change of plans.

Psychoanalytic Theory

Although many practitioners include certain psychoanalytic constructs in terms of a partial perspective on human behavior, e.g., unconscious motivation, defense mechanisms, etc., few practitioners utilize a pure psychoanalytic orientation in their work. If a teacher or counselor used a pure psychoanalytic orientation, then he would come to the inescapable conclusion that there is no need for vocational guidance or vocational counseling, per se. Similarly, there would be no place for occupational information. Therapy would have a "psychological" rather than "vocational" emphasis. Vocational indecision and vocational maladjustment would be viewed as symptoms of more fundamental psychological difficulty and would be dealt with through the use of traditional psychoanalytic techniques. Free association, hypnosis, probing, interpretation, dream analysis, and related techniques would be employed. Therapy would be a long and extensive process and the vocational theme would be either absent or very greatly deemphasized. Furthermore, the therapy would probably occur in the context of private practice rather than in an educational setting.

Sociological Theories

The sociological theories offer only very general guidelines for practice. The general theme of the sociological perspective is that pervasive economic and sociological factors or accidental (chance) factors limit the range of occupational choice. Presumably, traditional guidance procedures including the use of educational and occupational information with sociological perspective could be helpful in assisting the individual to make choices within the absolute limits of his unique situation. An important contribution of sociological theory is a sensitivity to the impact of restricted familial perspectives and the potentially limiting influence of various sociocultural mores on the individual's level of aspiration, his perception of the value of formal education, the perception of what constitutes appropriate occupational choice, and the perceived nature of success, advancement, satisfaction, etc. The sociological theories also highlight the need for compensatory education and the special needs of divergent minority groups if they are to move into the mainstream of the educational system, the occupational structure, and American life in general. The strategy of Project Head Start and New York City's Higher Horizons Project reflects a sensitivity to the need to bring the child from a minority group background into contact with representative thought and general experiences of the dominant social groups.

Need Theories

A practitioner who chose to use a need theory of occupational choice such as that of Hoppock or Roe would emphasize the role of work in satisfying the individual's needs as he tried to help that person to choose a job. Using Roe's theory, for example, the practitioner would gather a great deal of background data, particularly about his childhood. A determination would be made in terms of whether the person's orientation is toward or not toward people. A method of identifying and measuring the intensity of the person's needs would be employed. Since Roe states that both socioeconomic factors and ability influence occupational choice, these factors would also be assessed. Occupational information would be extensively used in order to show how each occupation could be used to satisfy particular needs. For example, while the occupations of psychiatrist and missionary both could satisfy social needs, the former job would satisfy the need for high financial reward much more adequately than the latter job. Presumably, the counseling interview would be the primary vehicle for help. A primary practical limitation of using Roe's theory as a basis for practice is that in working with adolescents and adults a determination of the early parent-child relationship (home climate) is necessary. Current methods for determining the nature of the early parent-child relations are questionable in terms of their validity and reliability as clinical instruments.

If Hoppock's formulation were used as a basis for practice, there would also be an emphasis upon helping the individual to know his interests, abilities, and needs. Furthermore, as in the case of practice based upon Roe's theory, the practitioner would emphasize how occupations can satisfy needs. More than any other need theorist, Hoppock has stressed the need to use occupational information to increase the probability that the person would make a satisfactory vocational decision, i.e., one in which he would enter an occupation which would satisfy his needs.

An Example of an Integrated Approach to Vocational Guidance

Rationale

An important aspect of the rationale for guidance is a perspective on the nature of education. In general, the task of education is defined in part by society and in part by the educational institution itself. In the broadest sense, education is a formal institution charged with the task of assisting the family and other segments of society with the socialization of youth. The general goal of education is threefold: (a) the socialization of youth, (b) the advancement of knowledge, (c) service to the community. The school operates by means of a fourway division of labor which includes the administrative function, the instructional function, the personnel function, and the ancillary function.

> Guidance is the systematic, professional process of helping the individual through educative and interpretive procedures to gain a better understanding of his own characteristics and potentialities and to relate himself more satisfactorily to social requirements and opportunities in accord with social and moral values. (Mathewson, 1962, p. 141)

Thus, guidance is a specialized process for implementing the general goals of the educational system by means of the utilization of the principles and techniques of the behavioral sciences and other related disciplines to individuals and groups of students, parents, and staff. The guidance practitioner is an educator who uses insights and techniques from various source fields to achieve his goals. The activities of guidance can be categorized as follows (Klopf, 1963):

1. Individual work with students.
2. Group work with students.
3. Individual and group work with staff.
4. Individual and group work with parents.
5. Working with the community.
6. Assembling data about students.
7. Providing information about opportunities.

The guidance program is predicated upon certain assumptions and while they are not always made explicit, a clear statement of these assumptions is useful in understanding the meaning of guidance and its place in the total scope of the educational endeavor.

1. Students need help in getting information which they might not be able to discover for themselves without paying an extremely high price in time, money, or effort. This need includes:
   a. Information about personal characteristics such as potential aptitudes, directions of interest, and motivations.
   b. Information about educational opportunities, occupational requirements, and available social services.
   c. Information about appropriate ways of behaving in various situations.
2. Students need help in adjusting to social requirements, meeting problems as they arise, overcoming weaknesses, and making plans for the future.
3. It is beneficial both for the individual and for the society when the individual achieves success and satisfaction in education, in his work, and in other aspects of his life.
4. Since there are so many alternative courses of action open to individuals, choice must be made; planning and looking ahead is beneficial for the individual in this process of choice.
5. The individual has an innate urge to make something of himself, to strive, and to grow.
6. The worth and dignity of the individual is a prime concern of guidance.
7. Although guidance assists individuals toward certain socially desirable goals, the ultimate decision in a situation rests with the individual.
8. The school may unknowingly interfere with the development of the individual, may aggravate existent problems, and even precipitate additional problems.
9. Guidance can attempt to create conditions in the individual and his environment which will facilitate his maximum development.
10. Literature and research in human development in the behavioral sciences constitute a basic for theory and practice in education and a developmental approach to guidance.
11. Processes in guidance can be so arranged in terms of timing and sequence that a later phase of development can be understood in the light of a former phase.
12. Many general techniques can be adapted to a developmental orientation to guidance, e.g., counseling, testing, etc.
13. The emphasis in guidance should not be upon dealing with

surface traits (symptoms) but upon causes, i.e., guidance should focus on dynamics behind behavior.

14. The student can learn about the factors that underlie behavior and can apply these learnings to others, to his own actions, and to the guiding of his own development.

15. When the individual understands himself and can formulate a plan of life that is best suited to him, he will be more satisfied and make a better contribution to society than he would without such a plan.

Guidance can be implemented as a group of services. These services attempt to assist the individual toward maximal development and a well-integrated personality. Counseling plays a major role in the total program and constitutes one of the major functions of the total guidance program. Although the major focus of the program is on the prevention of problems in individuals and upon the development of individual potential, there is another emphasis on the general adjustment of the individual through remedial assistance. Guidance processes are carried on in order to achieve the goals of the guidance program. There are long-term goals which tend to be abstract, such as the following. "The purpose of guidance is to improve the capacity of the individual to understand self and environment and to deal with self-situational relations with greater personal satisfaction and social usefulness in the light of social and moral values (Mathewson, 1962)." The concepts of psychosocial crises (Erikson), developmental tasks (Havighurst), and vocational developmental tasks (Super) can be used as vehicles for identifying short-term and intermediate-range goals of guidance, thereby providing cues in terms of the nature and dynamics of guidance practices which will facilitate the realization of desired goals (Zaccaria, 1965). Thus, psychosocial crises, developmental tasks, and vocational developmental tasks, i.e., environmental tasks, constitute some reference points in the course of human development upon which the teacher, the guidance worker, and other school personnel can focus their attention.

Vocational Guidance Practices in the Elementary School

The general environmental tasks of the elementary school years are those of achieving a sense of initiative and industry. In terms of vocational development, Havighurst (1953) describes the nature of the task as that of acquiring a store of concepts sufficient for thinking effectively about ordinary occupational matters. Stated in general terms, the long-term goal for the vocational development of the child in the elementary school is the creation of a readiness within each individual for the major exploratory activities of the junior high school and the senior high school. If the goal of achieving readiness is viewed as a fundamental goal, some aspects of this general goal or environmental task would be as follows (Kitch, 1953):

1. The recognition that all citizens of a democratic society are expected to be workers and therefore should select an occupation.
2. The recognition of the social value of all necessary work.
3. A familiarity with the different occupations followed by people in the pupil's own community.
4. An understanding of how different jobs influence individual living patterns.
5. An understanding of the relation of individual interest and abilities to the types of activities in different jobs.
6. An understanding of the pupil's own personal-social qualities.

Direct linkages can be made between the general guidance goal of helping the student to acquire a store of concepts sufficient for thinking about ordinary occupational matters and the more specific and immediate tasks. The teacher is the key person in the guidance program at the elementary level of education, with the guidance worker playing a largely consultative role. Focusing upon the role of the teacher and the vocational aspects of guidance, it can be seen that many regular classroom activities can be adapted to guidance and guidance-related activities. Social studies can serve as an illustration of a subject in the elementary school which can be easily adapted to many kinds of activities related to vocational guidance. Adaptations can be minor and still contribute greatly to the goals of guidance. The environmental task (a short-term goal of guidance) of helping the student to achieve a familiarity with the different occupations followed by people in the pupil's own community can be utilized to demonstrate some possible kinds of linkages which can be made between the classroom instructional phase of education and the guidance function. Norris (1963) notes, for example, that the elementary teacher in kindergarten through grade 3 can utilize an "Occupations in the Home and Community" approach as a major theme. Class helpers, games, field trips, class discussion, audio-visual aids, bulletin boards, poems, and various studies are general methods for carrying on vocational guidance within the social studies framework. In the second grade Norris suggests "Community Helpers" as a specific theme. The study and discussion of protection (police, fireman), food (grocer), shelter (carpenter, plumber, electrician), and products (businessman) is described. Occupational guessing games, occupational riddles, and the meanings of names (Cook, Taylor, Butler, etc.) are suggested as useful activities for this age. The study of industries can be the general theme for grades 4 through 6. The above-outlined program is geared to the widening scope of the child's world of realities. Keeping in mind that the general vocational environmental task for the child during the early elementary school years is that of acquiring a store of concepts for thinking effectively about ordinary occupational matters, the guidance and guidance-related activities described above can be seen as a rather short-term strategy. Norris' suggestions for typical activities articulate with the distant goals of guidance when viewed within the structure of developmental tasks.

Numerous approaches to elementary guidance have been proposed in the literature (Zaccaria, 1965). Each has its own inherent advantages and disadvantages. The term "child development consultant" has received rather wide attention in recent years to distinguish this type of practitioner from the traditional guidance counselor at the secondary level of education. Some typical vocationally related activities of the child development consultant might be as follows:

1. Locating, organizing, and supplying teachers with appropriate occupational materials.
2. Assisting teachers in the understanding and presentation of occupational materials.
3. Consulting with teachers about human relations in their own classrooms.
4. Consulting with teachers about student adjustment problems.
5. Taking part in case conferences.
6. Speaking and/or leading discussions in individual classrooms, groups or classrooms, and assemblies.
7. Meeting with teachers and parents in joint conferences.
8. Acting as a referral agent for teachers and administrators.
9. Testing and counseling.
10. Providing counseling and admistering tests.

Vocational Guidance Practices in the Junior High School

Typically, the student who enters the junior high school having gone through the type of developmental guidance program outlined above will have mastered the developmental tasks of achieving a familiarity with the basic concepts and attitudes necessary for the mastery of vocational developmental tasks of the adolescent period. If the guidance practices throughout the elementary school years have been based upon the developmental status of the pupil, and if an attempt has been made in the elementary school to provide a program of enriched experiences whereby the individual can begin to make preparations for his vocational development long before the actual crisis arises, then the individual will enter the junior high school with some basic attitudes and understandings which constitute a foundation for vocational guidance practices in early adolescence. Whereas the guidance worker in the elementary school plays a largely consultative role as a resource person for the teacher, the guidance worker in the junior high school plays a dual role. He is both a consultant to teachers and a counselor of students. Thus, he is called a guidance counselor. A comprehensive and well-balanced program of developmental guidance for the adolescent student emphasizes this dual role for the guidance practitioner.

The general process of vocational development during the adolescent years has been described by Super (1963) in terms of the individual being faced with a problem (vocational developmental task) of crystallizing a tentative and generalized vocational preference. This task is mastered within the broader context of seeking an identity. As a result of occupational exploration, patterns begin to emerge in the form of alternative courses of action and differential consequences. A tentative generalized crystallization of a vocational preference occurs and a decision is made. Action is taken as the decision becomes implemented. (This process is somewhat like the dynamics involved in the process of career problem solving as described by Tiedeman and his associates.)

Developmental guidance has two *foci* as it attempts to help the individual toward more adequate vocational development. There is a long-range effort directed toward helping the individual to make wise decisions relating to long-range vocational developmental tasks. A correlative effort is directed toward assisting the student at the actual choice or decision points. Focusing upon a single vocational developmental task will serve to illustrate how specific developmental guidance practices can be used at the junior high school level. One of the crucial steps of achieving the vocational developmental task of crystallizing a generalized vocational preference is that of utilizing community and school resources. Teachers and other school personnel can carry on the typical activities of a broad school-wide effort. The general science teacher, for example, can discuss the requirements for jobs and the typical work of people engaged in scientific occupations. The art teacher could bring her class to an art exhibition and talk to artists about their work. The same thing could be done by numerous other types of teachers, health staff, librarian, maintenance personnel, etc. Career days, career nights, PTA programs, movies, filmstrips, occupational information, group guidance activities, etc., can be adapted to meet the goals of a developmentally oriented program. Some dominant themes which could be a part of counseling, for example, are: the importance of work as an expression of self in a particular role, the significance of work in relation to general life style, and a general focus upon introspection and the projection of one's self into a future work role.

Speakers for career nights and career days could describe not only the typical aspects of work such as preparation, salary, working conditions, etc., but also on the effect of the job on their way of life. Similarly, the importance of the process of vocational development as that of developing and implementing a self-concept can be woven into the developmental counseling process. In the counseling in ninth grade, for example, the major themes would include a continued self-examination by the student of such aspects of his life as general directional goals, personal strengths and weaknesses, ideal vs. actual self-concept, style of adult life toward which he is striving, etc. The young adolescent is in a developmental stage of transition in which he is seeking to develop intrinsic attitudes of worth. But more adult status can emerge only as the adolescent is given the opportunity to make real choices. Thus, adolescent exploration is a process of developing and beginning to implement a realistic self-concept.

Many vocational guidance activities in the junior high school have short-range focus. In a gross sense, development is continuous and cumulative. Thus, the developmental guidance process is relatively continuous and cumulative. Vocational development, however, becomes most explicit at choice points when the individual must make decisions and is confronted with pressure to make a realistic commitment. The choice of a curriculum in the ninth grade represents such a choice point. Thus, at this point the student must specify some proximate choices, e.g., schedule of courses to be taken in the following year. He must begin to crystallize more distant decisions, e.g., whether he will go on to some form of post-high school education or training or whether he will enter the labor force. Meanwhile, distant decisions about an occupational choice per se may be even more tentative, being explored, crystallized, specified, and implemented in subsequent developmental stages. The choice of a curriculum in the ninth grade represents an immediate choice. It is a proximate or an immediate decision, a microcosm of a developmental task. On the other hand, crystallizing a generalized vocational preference is a more distant developmental task which can, when mastered, lead to entry into the work force in a job which will become part of an ongoing career. It is neither possible nor desirable to prevent all problems and crises in the life of the individual. The adolescent therefore will require assistance at the point of making some decisions. Individual and group counseling are two major approaches for helping individuals at the crisis or choice points. A unique characteristic of developmental counseling is that it has been preceded by a broad program of guidance aimed at providing help in developing adequate attitudes, values, understandings, and skills. Furthermore, the counseling tends to occur before the actual point of decision.

Developmental counseling with a long-range focus has several major goals. First, it assists the student in gaining self-insight. At choice points, developmental counseling helps the student to consider the entire range of his life experiences and the long-term consequences of the various potential course of action. Developmental counseling also attempts to facilitate the formation and application of a flexible and well-integrated orientation concerning the person and his place in the environment. The developmental counseling at choice points encourages self-analysis of all aspects of the individual's life experiences as they relate to the decision at hand and the subsequent behaviors relating to the implementation of the decision to be made.

Vocational Guidance Practices in the Senior High School

One of the long-range goals of developmental guidance in the senior high school is that of assisting the student to gain a sense of occupational identity. The immediate goal focuses upon helping the student with the task of specifying a vocational preference (Super, 1963). The older adolescent is expected to convert the generalized preference into a more specific preference. Two basic patterns emerge in the high school years depending upon whether high school represents terminal education for the individual or whether he goes on to post-high school education or training. A distinction now becomes necessary between vocational preference and vocational choice. Thus, a vocational preference refers to verbal behavior, e.g., an attitude of liking or disliking, and vocational choice signifies motor or instrumental behavior. The high school adolescent must both make a specific vocational preference and take initial steps to implement that preference.

The long-range focus of developmental guidance in the senior high school is a continuation of that begun in the elementary school years and extended into the junior high school years. For example, the inventory function (maintaining a cumulative record) can be carried on as an aspect of developmental guidance. The data are utilized in a unique manner, however. The contents of the cumulative folder (developmental record) can be utilized by both the guidance counselor and the student in order that the student can begin to use the data to develop a more realistic self-concept. The student might even begin a developmental folder of his own as an aid for clarifying his own thinking about himself and his vocational career. The guidance office could include a file cabinet to contain materials written by the student throughout his education. These materials could be used as aids for clarifying thought and selecting alternative courses of action. These materials might include student notes on counseling, themes, special student developmental record forms, etc.

Counseling can be the heart of the guidance program in the high school, but related activities also have an important function. Besides the traditional emphases, however, there can be the continued focus upon the individual's developing a vocational self-concept and subsequently implementing that self-concept through choice and action. The continued emphasis upon work as a means for implementing the self-concept, the constant fostering of reality testing, the use of probability tables for predicting success, and other practices can build on the foundations which have been laid in earlier years. Developmental group work at the senior high school level can be used as another approach for helping students to learn about the objective realities of the world of work and the subjective spheres of personal qualities. The dropout, the high school graduate, and the college-bound student each face somewhat different patterns of career development. The school is only one institution affecting the overall socialization of the youth. The student is only in the school for a relatively brief period of his total span of life. The student's contact with guidance and guidance-related activities is merely one aspect of his total school experience. It therefore behooves guidance programs to strive for maximum effectiveness. The integrated formulation and program of guidance such as that described above can be a significant factor in the total development of the individual.

Some Emerging Points of View

Current attempts to develop more useful theories of occupational choice and vocational development appear to be moving in several distinctly different directions. One group of theorists is attempting to extend and improve existing theories. Some efforts are being directed toward developing the general parameters of existing theories (e.g., Super, 1968a, b) while other theory-building has attempted to specify certain aspects of general theories. Thus, Gribbons and Lohnes (1964a, 1964b, 1968), for example, have been investigating the nature and dynamics of employing coping behaviors for becoming more vocationally mature. Another trend is evident in the work of other theorists who are attempting to utilize new approaches for extending certain limited aspects of existent theories. Searching for a more adequate method of predicting career patterns, Super (1968b) has investigated the use of lattice theory, Lohnes (1955) has studied chain theory, and Werts (1968) has attempted to apply path analysis. Despite the limited success of these studies, Super is optimistic about the ultimate development of adequate prediction models for his current global formulation of career pattern theory. Favoring the career tree prediction method developed by Flanagen and Cooley (1966) he notes,

> Whether the method [for predicting career patterns] will come from lattice theory, from path theory, or from something else is not yet clear. In five years we will no doubt have a better basis for judging, in ten years the data and the method will be available for use, and perhaps ten years later, in 1988, its application will be commonplace! (Super, 1968)

A *potpouri* of other emerging points of view is also evident. An existential framework has been utilized for the general process of counseling and guidance (e.g., Van Kaam, 1965; Johnson, 1967; Zaccaria, 1969) and for the process of vocational development (Simon, 1966). The systematic application of learning theory within a behavioristic point of view has been utilized for general counseling based upon the original work done by such theorists as Dollard and Miller (1950), Pepinsky and Pepinsky (1954), and Wolpe (1958). Learning theory has also been used as a framework for various aspects of vocational decision-making and the use of occupational information (Krumboltz and Thoreson, 1964; Krumboltz and Schroeder, 1965; Miler, 1968; O'Hara, 1968). Cognitive dissonance theory (Festiger, 1957) has also been adapted to explain vocational behavior (Hilton, 1962; Hershewson and Roth, 1966). Cognitive dissonance occurs when an individual's perception of his environment, e.g., vocational environment and his role in that environment are grossly at variance with external expectations. Thus, vocational behavior within a cognitive dissonance framework can be explained as follows: (a) a career-related event stimulates the individual's perception of the need to make a vocational decision, (b) the new demand changes the person's perception of the self-in-situation, i.e., it creates cognitive dissonance, (c) if the cognitive dissonance which is caused by the stimulus creates enough discomfort then the person will re-examine and change his beliefs and/or behavior, and last (d) to the extent that the resulting implementing behavior fails to decrease cognitive dissonance he will continue to seek new behaviors and to the extent that the implementing behavior reduces cognitive dissonance he will maintain the new behavior.

Reflecting the generally increasing influence of the behavioral sciences and interdisciplinary thought, another line of theory has begun to stress the ecology of human behavior, i.e., the study of the relationship between individuals and their environments. Guidance has been defined as the ecology of students (D. G. Danskin, et al., 1965). Another emerging emphasis appears to be that of environmental press, i.e., the impact of the situational (environmental) content upon individual behavior (Thistlewaite, 1960; Astin, 1965; Ford and Urban, 1965; Herr, 1965). These studies have begun to identify the influence of the individual's perception of environmental climate on educational and vocational choices as individual decisions reflect compromise or synthesis of individual inclinations and cultural opportunities.

Another type of effort to improve theories of occupational choice and vocational development is represented by the work of Flanagen who in 1960 began a major longitudinal study of almost half a million youth. Measures of aptitude, achievement, activity, occupational status, personality, etc., were administered and general demographic data were collected. This research effort (Project Talent) is now gathering the largest and most comprehensive pool of data regarding human talent ever attempted. Among the many goals of Project Talent are (a) the study of the factors affecting vocational choice and (b) the development of predictors of creativity and productivity. Although the major focus of this program is data gathering rather than actual theory-building per se, Project Talent offers a rich potential of data against which existent and future theory can be evaluated.

There are some trends and areas of inquiry which are not theories of occupational choice or vocational development per se, but nevertheless are either closely related to these theories or else have some implications for vocational theories. An important trend, for example, is the increased amount of leisure. Although the opportunity for more leisure is being disproportionately taken by certain segments of the work force, e.g., blue collar workers, many other sectors of the labor force will also have an increasing opportunity for leisure. Traditional statements of the goals of education have always recognized the need for the worthy use of leisure time (Cardinal Principles of Education), and sought the objective of self-realization through the development of esthetic and recreational interests (Educational Policies Commission Statement). To date, however, the realization that education and guidance should help the individual to use leisure has consisted more of a passing nod than systematic help. Certainly, as leisure time becomes more available, people will need (could use) help in learning to enjoy leisure activities more effectively. The major thrust in guidance has continued to be an emphasis on the unilateral theme of work rather than on the complementary or reciprocal work-leisure theme. A broad-gauged approach to the role and function of the guidance could include "recreational guidance" in addition to the traditional guidance themes.

Another area that has been largely overlooked is the provision of adequate guidance services for girls. Vocational theories are either general or male-centered. Vocational guidance has remained largely constrained by the prevailing stereotyped thinking that the only appropriate jobs for women are those of nurse, teacher, secretary, beautician, air line hostess, etc. The issue for the practitioner is whether or not he will attempt to help girls fulfill themselves occupationally to the same extent as males. To date, women in the world of work have constituted another minority or disadvantaged group.

And there is the broader and more pervasive task of providing all types of assistance for the disadvantaged, culturally different, and minority groups. Whether new techniques must be developed for these groups, whether current techniques need to be revamped, or whether existent strategies are sufficient without extensive revision would appear to be a secondary concern to the more fundamental issue of the nature and extent of the responsibility to this segment of our society.

The area of bibliotherapy, i.e., the use of imaginative and didactic literature for therapeutic purposes, has received increased attention in recent years. The theoretical and applied aspects of bibliotherapy have been described as a general therapeutic process (Zaccaria and Moses, 1968, 1969), as a part of the rehabilitation counseling process (Moses and Zaccaria, 1968), and as an extension of the traditional use of educational and occupational information service (Zaccaria and Moses, 1968). Contemporary vocational guidance seems to be infatuated along with much of the rest of our society with the "youth cult." The guidance effort has been extended to the elementary school setting and it has reached to the burgeoning junior college-community college movement. But little is being systematically done to help youth prepare for old age and retirement in either a vocational context or in a general style of life context.

There are two forces operating which are playing more potent roles in increasing change in our culture. Automation and cybernetics have already begun to change the role and function of the guidance practitioner, the meaning of work and leisure, and the day-to-day work in business, industrial, and educational settings. The second force is perhaps less apparent but at least as potent as automation and cybernation. This second force is that of the youth revolt and the generation gap. Youth seem to have been in an almost continuous state of unrest and upheaval since the dawn of Western civilization. Contemporary student movements, however, appear to be attacking the foundations of the meaning and usefulness of work, capitalism, materialism, vocational and social advancement, and our conventional reward system. Even the traditional bastions of motherhood, family, and the flag are under intense attack.

Summary and Prospectus

The general process of selecting, preparing for, entering, and advancing in the world of work may be viewed in a variety of ways. For purposes of presentation, the heterogeneous vocational theories have been described within the two broad contexts of choosing an occupation and proceeding with career development. Work has traditionally played a central role in man's life and while the general importance of work in individuals' lives appears to have decreased somewhat, it will undoubtedly continue as a significant determinant of the quality of man's life. Society cannot maintain or advance itself without work. Indeed, technological progress vastly increases the importance of work being done. The vast increase in the amount of work performed in our culture is evident when work production is viewed in traditional physical terms. One man can produce about 48 kilowatt-hours of work in one year. At the rate of 750 billion kilowatt-hours of electrical energy generated in the United States about a decade ago, the equivalent (at *that* time) of 85 slaves were at the disposal of each man, woman, and child (Piel, 1961).

Certainly we have made great progress in harnessing and utilizing physical energy for the production of more work and a higher materialistic standard of living. Yet technological progress does not inherently insure a correlative improvement in the psychological quality of human living. Contemporary America is an occupational-personal-social-moral-religious-cultural paradox. There is devastating poverty within general opulence. There is increasing maladjustment and greater opportunity for self-actualization. There is an alarming amount of hunger amid giant food surpluses. Life becomes more de-humanized as wages and working conditions improve. Jobs go unfilled as unemployment continues. Some youth as future workers seek a meaningful life through participation in the mainstream of American life, while other youth strive for other goals amid the growing minority of the protest-oriented alienated sector of our society. And the multidimensional racial crisis continues and becomes more serious as time goes on. The challenge for the field of counseling and guidance is to identify and carry out a helping role in the cross currents of American life. The challenge for the guidance practitioner is to seek worthy goals and to develop appropriate means for achieving these goals. A broadened concept of occupational choice or vocational development, work, and leisure can provide an anchor point for the practitioner's daily work.

BIBLIOGRAPHY

Allport, G. W., et al., *Study of Values* (Revised Edition). *Manual of Directions.* Boston: Houghton Mifflin Company, 1951.

Anastasi, Anne, *Psychological Testing.* New York: The Macmillan Company, 1959.

Astin, A. W., "Effects of Different College Environments on the Vocational Choices of High Aptitude Students." *Journal of Counseling Psychology,* Vol. 12, 1965, pp. 28–34.

Aubrey, R. F., "The Effect of Counselors on the Reward System of Teachers." *Personnel and Guidance Journal,* Vol. 45, 1967, pp. 1,017–1,020.

Barry, Ruth and Wolf, Beverly, *An Epitaph for Vocational Guidance.* New York: Bureau of Publications, Teachers College, Columbia University, 1962.

Bartlett, J., *The Shorter Bartlett's Familiar Quotations.* New York: Pocket Books, Inc., 1964.

Beck, C. E., *Philosophical Foundations of Guidance.* Englewood Cliffs, New Jersey: Prentice-Hall, Inc., 1963.

Bell, H. M., *Matching Youth and Jobs.* Washington, D.C.: American Council on Education, 1940.

Bell, H. M., *Youth Tell Their Story.* Washington, D.C.: American Council on Education, 1938.

Bingham, W. C., *Change of Occupation as a Function of the Regnancy of Occupational Self-Concepts.* Unpublished doctoral dissertation, Teachers College, Columbia University, 1966.

Bordin, E. S., "A Theory of Vocational Interests as Dynamic Phenomena." *Educational and Psychological Measurement,* Vol. 3, 1943, pp. 49–65.

Bordin, E. S., et al., "An Articulated Framework for Vocational Development." *Journal of Counseling Psychology,* Vol. 10, 1963, pp. 107–116.

Borow, H., "The Development of Motives and Roles." In L. W. Hoffman and M. L. Hoffman, eds., *Review of Child Development Research: Volume 2.* New York: Russell Sage Foundation, 1966.

Borow, H., ed., *Man in a World at Work.* Boston: Houghton Mifflin Company, 1964.

Brammer, L. M. and Shostrum, E. L., *Therapeutic Psychology.* Englewood Cliffs, New Jersey: Prentice-Hall, Inc., 1963.

Brill, A. A., *Basic Principles of Psychoanalysis.* Garden City, New York: Doubleday and Company, Inc., 1949.

Broudy, H., *Building a Philosophy of Education.* Englewood Cliffs, New Jersey: Prentice-Hall, Inc., 1961.

Buchler, J., *Charles Pierce's Empiricism.* New York: Harcourt and Brace Company, 1939.

Buehler, Charlotte, *Der Menschlische Lebenslauf als Psychologisches* Problem. Leipzig: Hirzel, 1933.

Butts, R. F., *A Cultural History of Western Education.* New York: McGraw-Hill Book Company, Inc., 1955.

Caplow, T., *The Sociology of Work.* Minneapolis, Minnesota: University of Minnesota Press, 1954.

Carkhuff, R. B., et al, "Do We Have a Theory of Vocational Choice?" *Personnel and Guidance Journal,* Vol. 46, 1967, pp. 335–345.

Carter, H. D., "The Development of Interest in Vocations." In N. B. Henry, ed., *Adolescence: 43rd Yearbook of the National Society for the Study of Education.* Chicago: Department of Education, University of Chicago, 1944 (a).

Carter, H. D., "The Development of Vocational Attitudes." *Journal of Consulting Psychology,* Vol. 8, 1940, pp. 185–191.

Carter, H. D., *Vocational Interests and Job Orientation.* Stanford: Stanford University Press, 1944 (b).

Coleman, J. S., *The Adolescent Society.* Glencoe: The Free Press, 1959.

Cribbin, J., "Critique of the Philosophy of Modern Guidance." *Catholic Educational Review,* Vol. 53, 1955, pp. 73–91.

Danskin, D. G., "Guidance: The Ecology of Students." *Personnel and Guidance Journal,* Vol. 44, 1965, pp. 130–135.

Davidson, P. E. and Anderson, H. D., *Occupational Mobility in an American Community.* Stanford, California: Stanford University Press, 1937.

Dollard, J. and Miller, N. E., *Personality and Psychotherapy.* New York: McGraw-Hill Book Company, Inc., 1950.

Drasgow, J., "Occupational Choice and Freud's Overdeterminism." *Vocational Guidance Quarterly,* Vol. 6, 1957, pp. 67–68.

English, H. B. and English, Ava C., *A Comprehensive Dictionary of Psychological and Psychoanalytic Terms.* New York: Longmans, Green and Company, Inc., 1958.

Erikson, E. H., *Childhood and Society.* New York: W. W. Norton Company, 1950.

Festiger, L. A., *A Theory of Cognitive Dissonance.* Stanford, California: Stanford University Press, 1957.

Flanagan, J. C. and Cooley, W. W., *Project Talent: One-Year Follow-Up Studies.* Pittsburgh: University of Pittsburgh, 1966.

Super, D. E., *Vocational Development Theory: Persons, Positions, and Processes.* Mimeographed, 1968b.

Super, D. E. and Overstreet, P. L., *The Vocational Maturity of Ninth-Grade Boys.* New York: Teachers College, Columbia University, Bureau of Publications, 1960.

Super, D. E., et al., *Career Development: Self-Concept Theory.* Princeton, New Jersey: College Entrance Examination Board, 1963.

Super, D. E., et al., *Vocational Development: A Framework for Research.* New York: Teachers College, Columbia University, Bureau of Publications, 1957.

Terman, L. M., *Genetic Studies of Genius.* Stanford: Stanford University Press, 1925.

Thistlewaite, D. L., "College Press and Changes in Study Plans of Talented Students." *Journal of Educational Psychology,* Vol. 51, 1960, pp. 222–234.

Tiedeman, D. V., "Decision and Vocational Development." *Personnel and Guidance Journal,* Vol. 40, 1961, pp. 15–20.

Tiedeman, D. V. and O'Hara, R. P., *Career Development: Choice and Adjustment.* New York: College Entrance Examination Board, 1963.

Titiev, M., *The Science of Man.* New York: Holt, Rinehart, and Winston, Inc., 1963.

Van Kaam, A., "Counseling from the Viewpoint of Existential Psychology." In R. L. Mosher, et al., eds., *Guidance: An Examination.* New York: Harcourt, Brace, and World, Inc., 1965.

Whyte, W. H., *The Organization Man.* Garden City, New York: Doubleday and Company, 1957.

Williamson, E. G., "Vocational Counseling: Trait and Factor Theory." In B. Stefflre ed., *Theories of Counseling.* New York, McGraw-Hill Book Company, Inc., 1965.

Winn, A. C., *You and Your Lifework: A Christian Choice for Youth.* Chicago: Science Research Associates, 1963.

Wolpe, J., *Psychotherapy by Reciprocal Inhibition.* Stanford: Stanford University Press, 1958.

Zaccaria, J. S., "Developmental Guidance: A Concept in Transition." *The School Counselor,* Vol. 13, 1966, pp. 226–229.

Zaccaria, J. S., "Developmental Tasks: Implications for the Goals of Guidance." *Personnel and Guidance Journal,* Vol. 44, 1965, pp. 372–375.

Zaccaria, J. S., "Guidance Implications of Concepts from the Field of Culture and Personality." *Personnel and Guidance Journal,* Vol. 46, 1967, pp. 907–910.

Zaccaria, J. S., "Some Aspects of Developmental Guidance within an Existential Concept." *Personnel and Guidance Journal,* Vol. 48, 1969, pp. 440–445.

Zaccaria, J. S., "The Varied Contributions of Elementary School Guidance." *Education,* Vol. 86, 1965, pp. 75–77.

Zaccaria, J. S. and Moses, H. A., "Bibliotherapy: An Extension of the Information Service in School Guidance." *Guidance Journal,* Vol. 5, 1967, pp. 147–156.

Zaccaria, J. S. and Moses, H. A., *Facilitating Human Development through Reading.* Campaign, Illinois: Stipes Publishing Company, 1969.

Zilboorg, G., "The Problem of Constitution in Psychopathology." *Psychoanalytic Quarterly,* Vol. 3, 1934, pp. 339–362.

INDEX

ABCDEFGHIJ— A —7654321O